A
TASTE
FOR
ADVENTURE

A Culinary Odyssey Around the World
ANIK SEE

SEAL PRESS

A TASTE FOR ADVENTURE: A Culinary Odyssey Around the World

Introduction copyright © 2001 by Anik See

Published by Seal Press
An Imprint of Avalon Publishing Group Incorporated
161 William St., 16th Floor
New York, NY 10038

First Seal Press edition, January 2002. Original Canadian edition published under the title *A Fork in the Road*,
copyright © Anik See, 2000. All rights reserved including the right of reproduction in whole or in part in any
form. This edition published in arrangement with CDG Books Canada, Inc. The Macmillan Canada logo is a
trademark or a registered trademark in the United States and/or other countries under exclusive license to CDG
Books Canada, Inc. Used by permission.

Cover design by Trina Stahl
Text design by Tania Craan
Cover photograph by Paul Edmondson/Image Bank
Author photo by Pam Ferrazzutti; All interior photography by Anik See, with the exception of Georgian photos
by Aaron Riggs, Alex Tilson and Doug Sage; Bali photo by Joanna See; Busheer, Iran photo by Doug Sage
Spanish revision by Juan Pablo Lewinger

Excerpt p.199 reprinted with the permission of Simon and Schuster, NY, from *Mexico* by Alice Adams.
Introduction by Jan Morris. Introduction copyright © 1990 by Jan Morris. Excerpt p.177 reprinted with
the permission of Macmillan Publishers, Ltd., London, from *The Road to Oxiana* by Robert Byron. Copyright
© 1937 by Robert Byron. Excerpt p.119 reprinted with the permission of Peter Owen, Ltd., from *Adventures
in Caucasia* by Alexandre Dumas. Copyright © 1859 by Alexandre Dumas. Excerpt p.26 reprinted with the
permission of Random House Archive and Library, London, from *In Patagonia* by Bruce Chatwin. Copyright
© 1977 by Bruce Chatwin. Excerpt p.136 reprinted with the permission of Mayday Management, from
"Full Circle with Michael Palin." Episode 5. Excerpt p.61 reprinted with the permission of Crown Publishing
Group, from *A Taste of the Far East* by Madhur Jaffrey. Copyright © 1993 by Madhur Jaffrey.

ISBN: 1-58005-065-4

Library of Congress Cataloging-in-Publication Data has been applied for.

9 8 7 6 5 4 3 2 1

Printed in Canada

Distributed to the trade by Publishers Group West

This book is dedicated to my grandparents, who not only handed down their thirst for new places, but also passed on their spirit of adventure and a healthy desire for being humbled by different cultures. These are the only things a traveller should leave home with.

ACKNOWLEDGMENTS

It is said that writing is the loneliest of the arts, but writing a book is never a solitary affair. Without the help of editors and publishers and designers, these stories would be nothing. Without the help of friends and family, this experience would be meaningless.

For encouragement, constructive criticism, eyes, and patience, thanks to Doug, Crispin, Kevin, Alex, Tracy, Julian, Dan, Wendy, Steven, Alan, Roger, Tim, Laura, Rick and Andrew.

For unwavering support and enthusiasm, thanks to Sue and Bob Adams, Carol, Mike, Manfred, and my entire family, all of whom taught me to do things creatively, and right.

Enormous thanks to Jennifer for believing in this and to all those with the Macmillan imprint at CDG Books Canada for an incredible amount of support, creativity, and faith.

Incalculable thanks to all of the characters on the road who provided me with the material for this book. I have tried to include all of you and by relaying your stories, hope I have done justice to the unbridled hospitality, wisdom, and warmth you gave a complete stranger.

And finally, I owe an eternal thank you to James, who taught me that life is too short to eat bad food, and that there is something exciting to be found in the dullest of places—and whose vivacity has been instilled in me, too.

CONTENTS

INTRODUCTION

I'm at my mother's house, looking in her address book for the phone number of a family friend, and I notice that under A, instead of the usual listing of names and addresses, there are instead just names of places: *San Francisco, Montauk, hotel in Shiraz, Geneva, Tblisi—ask for Babu, Mexico, West Coast,* etc., with a phone number after each. It takes a while, but it slowly dawns on me that these are the phone numbers of all the various places I've lived in or been to. The A in my mother's address book is reserved for *Anik.*

When I ask her about it, she laughs, tells me it's impossible to keep track, that it's the only way for her to remember where I am. This surprises me. I don't think of myself as particularly transient or forever moving; I'm just interested in other places. She says, "But don't you notice that when you talk to people, they don't ask *how* you are, but *where* you are? It's difficult to keep up with you." I hadn't noticed. Travelling seems so natural to me.

This book covers various journeys I took in the last ten years, most of them solo, and most by bicycle. I was working in television then, on a food show in Canada called *The Urban Peasant,* and the schedule alternated between intensive and lax—we would work almost every day for three months, then have three months off. The sporadic pay did not make for luxurious living, but the schedule was great for travelling. I met my sister in Indonesia, went to the Middle East with my boyfriend Doug, and crammed the solo trips in between.

I didn't have any particular motivation for going to these places, other than simple curiosity; but what I found when I was there, anywhere, was that in every culture, no matter how rich or poor, no matter how remote or connected, food was offered as a communicator—as a form of welcome, as a form of hospitality. The less of the language I spoke, the more food would emerge to serve as a way of teaching this dusty foreign girl on a bike something about the place she was in.

In Chile, when I asked an old woman about Pinochet, she pushed still-warm cake into my hands as a response and turned away. In Iran, when we asked a young man leading us through a bazaar about the Shah and Khomeini, he kept dragging us into restaurants and tea shops. It was as though they were saying, "experience my culture first, through food, and then we can move on to politics." Food is a connector. Political discussions are tricky to negotiate; food, on the other hand, stays simple. It is a question of survival, and what better way to communicate than through the very thing that sustains us?

Where James Barber, the host of *The Urban Peasant*, was my mentor at home, while abroad, the people I met and came to know collectively merged into my travelling mentor. They took me under their wings, took the time to share their food and philosophies with me—perhaps because they delighted in my ill-planned but profound adventures. They recognized in me a desire to take a second, closer look; to leave with a better understanding of what surrounded me. In my own experience, rarely do we share such wisdom with our neighbors as we do with people we are likely to never see again. But at the same time, the traveller has the ability to teach us. Learning from her, we might even find ourselves motivated to jump over the edge ourselves and place our trust in landing somewhere—to get off the bus a stop early just for the hell of it, or to try speaking Spanish even though we are embarrassed by our pronunciation, or to try that thing hanging from the food stall that looks like a dried brain but which smells good and puts a look of ecstasy on the locals' faces.

This book is about encouraging people to seek that out—to step out of their comfortable worlds and plunge into something unknown— to get past the Western fear and assumption that beyond our "safe" borders lurk dark and seedy characters just waiting to take advantage of us. This book is about realizing that in places where culture is celebrated vivaciously, fear simply dissipates. The world is much more open-armed than we think.

⌇

Right now I'm sitting on a dock on the Rideau Canal in eastern Canada (Elgin in the A section of my mother's address book). I'm looking up, and in the sky there is the shiny glint of a jet airplane caught in the sun's grasp, pushing silently east; I'm thinking, there are four hundred people going somewhere else. I'm hoping that most of them realize the freedom of being 38,000 feet up and headed somewhere new. I want everyone on that plane to be on their way to a place they have always wanted to go—maps already perused and worn in the folds from curious fingers following streets, emergency cab fare handy in a coat pocket—but intending to walk everywhere, to soak everything in. I want everyone to have already envisioned the park bench or alleyway or restaurant where they will sit or walk or close their eyes and taste something they have never tasted before and realize that they are finally here, that they have been waiting for so long and they are finally here. The prospect of others experiencing a culture new to them, no matter how shiny or raw, makes me dreamy. Wouldn't that be something? A planeload of people going somewhere they've always wanted to go, doing something they've always wanted to do. Jumping.

The plane is almost out of sight now; the sun is setting, and I catch one last flash of wing before it dissolves into dusk. But the electricity that those travellers high above me feel because they're jumping—taking a risk—is churning inside me. And I am happy for them. I am as excited as they are.

Anik See
August 2001

MALAYSIA & SINGAPORE

I am on the local train, on the milk run from Bangkok to the Malaysian border, slipping south through slums in a post-dusk haze, the kind of landscape you only see from train windows. My brain has been numbed, stunned by the way Bangkok manages to function with seemingly great efficiency amid a perpetual traffic jam, the contrast of slums and penury amidst the shininess of purpose and economy and affluence. From what I have heard, Malaysia promises a simpler existence, and I settle onto a wooden bench on the train with a slower pace already making its way through me. Local travellers welcome me, offering a mouthful of rice, or a tiny finger banana, smiling when I accept.

The farther we get from Bangkok the more intense the parade of food. Officials walk up and down the length of the train (about twenty-five cars long) offering water, Coca-Cola, Mekong whisky, beer, soda, rice, eggs, chicken, soup, juice. Children appear out of nowhere at every stop. First I hear the sound of their feet pounding on gravel, running alongside the tracks, then I see a glint of their plastic-wrapped wares, held up to the train's open windows: almond cookies or eggs cooked in sweet dough, all wrapped in yellow cellophane and tied with thin red ribbons, looking gorgeous, or sweets folded into bags made of old computer printouts. The kids run along the tracks, holding their packages up to hands stretched out of windows, screaming prices up and down the length of the train, grabbing cash from one hand and pressing the goods into the other, almost as though it is illegal.

Women board the train tottering under the weight of huge wicker baskets mounded with stuffed chicken legs and wings, fresh fruit, sticky rice folded into pink banana flowers or wrapped in pandan leaves. They ride the train until their basket is half-empty or until everyone's appetite has not only been satiated but exhausted. They hop off the train to catch the next one back.

The amount of food increases with the lateness in the evening. By three in the morning, the whole train is famished, despite the fact that not a single hour has gone by when any of us have not put something into our mouths; it is the kind of ravenous hunger that comes from a day of constant grazing and a sudden late-night alertness. The flavour of an elegantly charred chicken leg at dawn cannot be put into words. Gradually, the sun's rays begin to lick the bottoms of low-lying clouds and sweep through the glistening rice paddies on either side of the train, and I fall asleep to the sounds of children clapping and smacking their lips.

≈

At the border, I stand under the tin roof of a shack at customs and watch a wall of water descend from the sky. A sudden torrential storm has everyone pulled outside, mesmerized. Even the guards lose their scowls and smile at this spectacle of water. We are staring at nothing. The sheet of rain has blocked everything from our view, the red clay road, the green palms lining it, the cinderblock building a few yards from us, the black clouds that gave birth to this, now heaving with thunder, all of it obliterated by this wall of water. The Malay woman standing beside me giggles as the ground shakes. Eyes widen and children squeeze themselves into the hollows of their parents' legs, grabbing fabric with tiny sticky fingers.

≈

I make my way to Penang, where it is hard for me to imagine that this was once a bastion of R&R for American soldiers fighting in Vietnam. Remarkably, there is no trace of that left. The place reverberates with the multiculturism that is Malay, the result of a period of British administration, when East Indians and Chinese were brought over to work in mines and on plantations. Today, men wearing Indian smocks and sarongs walk down the street behind old, round women in Mao suits and straw peaked hats; a young woman wearing a chador and veil trips over young, blond children in Spanish T-shirts playing jacks. I feel strangely at home here.

I lean out of the window of my room above a bustling street, drinking in new colours made dusty by midday sunshine, and breathe in a labyrinth of smells: the salt of the Andaman Sea, whose whitecaps I glimpse over some low-roofed buildings; the exhaust of endless mopeds and buses; the stench of durian from the vendor below me who has been expelled from the lobby of the luxury hotel next door; the sharp heat of chilis fried in oil from the open restaurant across the street. I watch a young Sikh man wipe down all the tables in the restaurant, then stand in the breeze in the doorway, smoking and looking up and down the street for friends. He finishes his cigarette, flicks it out into the traffic, and ducks into the restaurant just in front of his first customer.

I walk downstairs, past the woman selling durian, and cross the road. I go into the restaurant and sit down. The young man approaches, bringing a glass of water and asking me in Malaysian what I'd like. I raise my palms up, looking helpless, and he laughs. He pats my shoulder and disappears into the kitchen. In a few moments he returns with a platter of buttery, flaky flatbread and a bowl of what looks like puréed yellow lentils. Sitting down across from me, he uses the delicate fingers of his right hand to show me how to tear pieces of the bread off, form them into a scoop, and use them to spoon the lentils into my mouth. He watches me as I eat, smiling at my reaction to the bread's simple, rich, dissolving texture, and laughing when the cumin, cardamom and onion seeds in the lentil stew explode on my tongue. Through the whole meal, he sits with me, quietly sketching long-plumed birds on the inside covers of my journal. He opens the book to the last page I have written on and begins to read words at random out loud: "*landscape... clear green sea... wall of rain... stands in the breeze in the doorway.*" He gives me back my journal, then gets up and brings over a menu, in Malaysian. From it I read words out loud: "*rendang... santen... rempah... asam...* " He points to something on the menu, *dalcha*, and grabs the bowl that the lentil stew was in. He runs his fingers along the words *roti chanai* and points to the few flakes of flatbread left on the plate. In my journal, he carefully writes the names in the space after my last entry. I ask him how much I can pay him and he closes his eyes. Nothing. He gets up and motions me to bring my journal and follow him.

Jagjit takes me into the kitchen where the cook is pounding some spices in a large mortar. The pestle he is using is the size of my forearm. The cook looks up at me and nods as Jagjit speaks to him. He keeps nodding and then motions for me to stand in front of the mortar. He hands me the pestle and asks me to keep pounding while he goes to the back corner of the kitchen, where he fetches a large stainless steel bowl covered with a cloth. He pulls the cloth back to show me that the bowl is filled with small balls of well-oiled dough. After he removes two of them, he covers the bowl and again sets it aside. He throws one of the balls of dough to Jagjit and they both flatten them with their hands on a large table. When the dough is as large as a pancake, each of them takes his dough into his hands and flicks it out, hanging onto an edge, stretching it. They rotate and flick, rotate and flick, rotate and flick until each of the pieces has turned into a large, translucent sheet of pastry about two feet in diameter. Jagjit folds the edges of his piece into the centre, then takes the cook's piece and does the same, making two neat squares.

The cook splashes some water on a hot griddle, then brushes it with ghee, a clarified butter used in Indian cuisine. He throws both rotis on the griddle and turns them every thirty seconds or so until they are nicely browned. He brushes more ghee on top to crisp them up, then places them on a plate for us to eat.

We pull the hot bread away in strips, blow on it, and drop it in our mouths. It dissolves into nothing but a whisp of buttery flavour. As we eat, the cook looks at what I have done in the mortar. He pounds it a little more, then sets it aside. Tossing me a ball of dough, he tells me to make a roti. He jerks his fingers out, showing me the wrist flick motion and pushes my elbow, encouraging me to try it. I flatten the dough, then grab a side and flick it out. He nods approval and I keep flicking, but of course my roti is much lumpier and more oblong than theirs were. Nevertheless, he is very patient with me and watches me while he puts together other orders that Jagjit has taken. A couple of hours and a few more balls of dough later, I finally have something that he can serve. The cook calls Jagjit back and shows him. Jagjit laughs, claps me on the shoulder, and cheers while I wipe sweat from my forehead. In good humour, the cook points at the clock and tells me to show up for work tomorrow at 9 a.m.

Jagjit sends me back across the street with four rotis and tells me to come for a free dinner. I give two of the warm rotis to the woman selling durian in the doorway of the guesthouse I am staying at. She thanks me with a smile. I give the others to some kids playing in the street, who have inhaled them before I even turn away. I move slowly up the stairs to my perch above this bustling street on Penang.

⌒

I spend a few days exploring Penang, wandering through its alleys and streets, saturated with the saltiness of the ocean breeze, enveloped in Malaysia's relaxed, open character. I feel welcomed everywhere. No matter where I go, people greet me with smiling faces and affectionate touches. Still, there comes a time when I feel the need to move on, and as I consider my next move, I wonder if I will encounter the same friendliness in the more southern and eastern reaches of the country. On the morning of my departure, I go over to Jagjit's restaurant to say goodbye. The place is not open yet, but Jagjit is inside and when he sees me in the doorway he pulls me inside and offers me some tea. We talk via hand gestures for a while and then I tell him that I'm leaving, heading south. He takes my journal and writes his address inside the front cover, under one of the birds he has drawn. We stand, and he pats me on the shoulders and wishes me luck. I cross the street but turn when I hear him shout. He makes frantic hand movements for me to wait, as though he has just realized something, then rushes inside. He picks up the phone and speaks into it excitedly. I cross the street again and by the time I am back at the restaurant, he has hung up and is waving for me to come inside. He tells me to wait for a moment. The cook arrives and coaxes me into the back to help him make some *rempah*, or spice paste, the same paste he had me pound a few days ago. I pound garlic into a purée while he chops some shallots and red chilis. He adds the shallots, some thinly sliced lemongrass, candlenuts, the chilis, and galangal to my garlic and encourages me to keep going. After a lot of pounding and stirring, the mixture suddenly comes together and becomes smooth. The cook adds a bit of dried shrimp paste and some oil, motions for me to stir it all together and then tells me to stop. What will he use it for, I ask him, and he tells me that this is his *rempah* supply for the whole day, the spicy base for most of the curry dishes and soups on his menu.

Jagjit comes into the kitchen and brings me out to the front. A woman dressed in an Indian tunic and trousers stands at the entrance to the restaurant, sunglasses perched on top of her head. She holds out her hand. "Hello, I'm Surinder… " she says. Jagjit stands beside us and grins and executes a series of quick bows. Surinder laughs.

"Jagjit told me on the phone that you are leaving today." I nod. "Good. I can give you a ride as far as Marang. Is that all right?"

I am a little taken aback. "Yes, of course. I.... This is unexpected."

I dash back into the kitchen to say goodbye to the cook, run across the street to grab my bag, wave goodbye to the woman selling durian on the stoop, and shake Jagjit's hand. Surinder and I drive off in a flurry.

We drive south on the main road to Kuala Lumpur for a while, passing enormous clear-cut plots of red earth. Surinder tells me about her family, about how they came to Malaysia from India when she was ten, and how now she has relatives scattered across the whole country, which is why she is going to Marang. She tells me more about Jagjit, who is her cousin.

We leave the clear-cut and twist high into the hills, looking onto terraced fields of green cut into lush segments of jungle. I ask her if she ever goes back to India, and she shrugs. "Sometimes. Not so often. I consider myself Malaysian, even though my childhood memories are all Indian." She pauses. "I still have family there, in Bombay, but when I am there, I feel like I am an outsider. When I am here," she looks over at me, "I feel Indian and Malaysian at the same time. And that is a good feeling."

"The best of both worlds?" I ask.

"Mmmmm..." She thinks. "Yes, in a way. I feel more accepted. No one on the street is judging me, looking at how much gold I am wearing or wondering what religion I am. I am assumed to be Malaysian, and I am Malaysian. But I still have my family here to remind me of my roots and the traditions we have brought from India. There are not so many countries where you can do that."

She asks me if it is like this in the West. More or less, I say, in cities. I tell her that I know the feeling she is talking about and that it is a wonderful one to have. "But," I say, "in the West, we seem to think that exporting our lifestyle is more important than celebrating culture."

Walking from village to village through the rice paddies

"What do you mean?"

"Well, westerners seem to have this notion that the way we do things is the right way, and that everyone else should be so fortunate as to live the way we do. But to me, a lifestyle of heavy consumerism seems to come at the expense of spirituality and cultural divergence. We lose our identity. We simply become consumers, not Canadians or Malaysians or Smiths or Jagjits. As westerners, we don't take the time to explore our ancestry or our traditions, so we lose a sense of who we are, and come to define ourselves by what we own instead. And we're exporting that all over the world. Drink Coke. Wear Calvin Klein. Listen to Céline Dion. Why? Why not engage ourselves in the colours of other cultures instead of promoting ours as the best?..." I look over at Surinder, who has her eyebrows raised.

"Sorry," I say. "My soapbox..."

"No, no, it's okay. You're right. The West promotes itself as having all the answers. And we believe it. But if you ask me, consumerism just seems to complicate things. I like a simple life. I don't ask for much, I don't impose on this world much, out of respect for its delicacy." She glances out the window as we enter another cut-block of carved red earth. "We're kind of screwing things up, right now."

"Yes," I say, "and we seem to think we're entitled to do that. We seem to be beset with a kind of arrogance of entitlement that has been brought on by consumerism."

"So what do we do?" Surinder asks.

"I don't know yet." We fall silent.

We turn off the main road onto a side route that takes us down towards the ocean in stepping plateaus. At the coast, thin stretches of white sand bring the mountains carefully into the sea. A rainstorm approaches and we pull over at a roadside café. As we step out of the car, the clouds let loose their first big tears onto our cheeks. The heavy blue-black clouds turn the palms and mountainsides into a fierce, lusty, emerald colour. Sheets of water slam onto the ground. The restaurant, like most in Malaysia, has no walls or windows—it is simply a kitchen and a bunch of tables set up under a zinc roof. We sit under it and watch, the rain so loud that it prevents conversation.

Surinder shouts over to me and asks if I have had murtabak yet. I shake my head. She orders two and then pokes me, pointing at the man behind me who is making Malaysian-style coffee. He has a large metal mug in one hand and a small metal cup in the other. He holds them close together then separates them quickly, as far as his arm span will let him, pouring the liquid from one into the other with incredible accuracy. Without spilling a drop, he does this back and forth for a minute or two, until the coffee is frothy and rich. He brings the cup over to me and starts making one for Surinder. There is a sting of ginger and whiff of cardamom in it, creamy and smooth.

The murtabak arrives and Surinder tells me that it is essentially roti, stuffed with mutton or beef or eggs. It is even more delicious than the roti I had at Jagjit's. When I bite into it, the bread dissolves into the meat, which is minced and spiked with cinnamon and cloves and Vietnamese mint. I roll it all around in my mouth, loath to swallow, but Surinder tells me I must, because it should be eaten hot. We laugh and joke with the coffee man through the meal, watching the rain pounding on the road and ripping fronds from the palms, and lift our feet when streams of water push themselves along the dirt floor of the restaurant.

The rain stops suddenly, without warning, and within minutes the sky has cleared completely. Not a cloud. Surinder and I watch, mesmerized by nature's fickleness. "I love this," she says. "It's my favourite time of the day." On the beach by the restaurant, two men pull up in a fishing skiff and drag what look like two marlins across the sand towards a barbecue pit. The men are soaked to the bone, laughing at the fortune of sudden rain, chatting happily as they try to find dry wood to prepare a fire. A good day's catch.

After leaving Surinder I spend a few days basking in the slow-paced villages of Malaysia's east coast, eventually making my way down to Kuala Lumpur. Compared to Bangkok, it too feels sleepy, structured; the traffic is civil and moves at a pace visible to the naked eye. Kuala Lumpur's residents seem content, less rushed, more likely to stop and talk to friends on the street. I stay in a place that overlooks the night market, a stretch of pedestrian-only stalls where it's possible to buy anything and everything, but most importantly, some of the best food in Malaysia.

I start out early, an hour before sunset, meandering through the wet market, where fresh fish and vegetables are sold, and where a constant spray of water keeps everything alive and crisp. Rattan baskets overflow with live blue crabs, anchovies, prawns and squid, stacks and stacks of leafy greens, pyramids of herbs and roots as far as the eye can see.

In quiet alleyways, old women in smocks and bare feet waddle quickly and with purpose, gathering last-minute items before all of Kuala Lumpur comes out to feast under the market's lights. The stalls are quiet, filled with young girls preparing food for the evening, expertly chopping and hacking vegetables with machetes twice the length of their arms. Fires are lit on the ground in the stalls and fanned with stiff banana or pandan leaves, oil is added to woks and the girls sit hunched by their fires, waiting for customers.

And suddenly, as though a whistle has sounded or a bell has been rung, the stalls are crammed with people, squinting at wares under strings of bare lightbulbs, bargaining with the hawkers. Woks sizzle, and the air is filled with murmurs of conversation and the exchange of gossip. I pass a stall that has tiny wooden cages, each with an insect in it, cicadas, I think. One of them buzzes as I pass, and the hawker laughs and flaps his hand at me, asking me if I want to buy it.

I enter the T-shirt and bootleg tape section, where rip-offs of western brand names (Channel, Hard Rock Cat, Rollex) flutter in a breeze and where George Michael, Led Zeppelin, and Sting blare out of speakers all at once, all around me. I move back into the food section, where I see a man hacking the outside husk off a coconut. He chops the nut in half and throws it into a machine that lurches and clatters and spits out shredded flesh into a bowl below. He takes some of the flesh and some of the milk, places it in a steel cup, adds ice and water and hands it over to me, telling me I should drink it. Gorgeous. My mother always told me that I didn't like coconut milk, and I consider telephoning her to tell her that she was wrong. Really wrong.

≈

Singapore is a slap in the face. The simpler life I saw in Malaysia is treated with disdain here. Commerce seems to be all that matters, and the city is a reminder of my soapbox, of western-style consumerism being sold overseas, in lieu of a respect for this country's now-distant culture. But squashed in between the glittery skyscrapers of Singapore are reminders of simplicity, seemingly kept underfoot by the power that money brings. Some of the world's oldest shacks still stand here, and these are where the best food in Singapore comes from.

It is a city of contrasts. If you stand on one street corner, you feel as though you could be in Dallas or Chicago, surrounded by nothing but glass and steel towers, pristine air-conditioned shopping centres full of boutiques beyond counting, billboards of the latest Hollywood films, exquisitely dressed office workers tripping across the street in Italian leather shoes, money, money, money. And if you turn and walk away from all that, peek around a corner, you realize that just a block away, the world changes. If you look under the perfectly woven carpet of glamorous Singapore, where

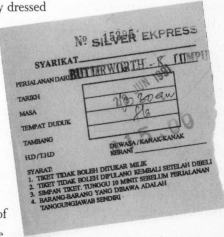

all the unsightly things are swept, you find the occasional street of rubble, or hastily built shelters from which dusty, wrinkled women sell wares from another era—Brylcreem, thick iron woks and cleavers, bottles of India ink, curlers, steel washboards—and from which scents of sweat and steam and sewage rise up to meet you.

I decide to walk from one end of the city core to the other to find those places, from its fragrant Indian quarter to the stalls by the water that sell Hainanese hot pot chicken, noodle soups of all kinds, and fresh juice made from sugar cane and starfruit.

I begin in Little India, where I lose myself in the back alleys for a couple of hours. I walk past piles and piles of spices: of vicious yellow turmeric; of tiny, fragrant pods of cardamom; of curiously shaped fenugreek. I watch a woman in Indian dress crouching by a large wok set over a fire in the middle of an alleyway. She is deep-frying pakoras and has a pot of *dalcha* going on the side. I notice that the *dalcha* being made here is different than the one I had on Penang. The woman adds fresh curry leaves, cilantro, and cinnamon bark to it and hands me a spoon for a taste. In all this heat and humidity, it is the most refreshing thing I can imagine. It is spicy and hot, but I immediately feel cooled. She grins at me and waggles her head, delighted at my reaction.

A few alleyways over, I stand by an old Tamil man who is pounding a mixture of whole spices into a powder for a woman, her own personal masala. After she tells him how much of which spices she wants in the mixture, he places them first on a cradle of solid rock and crushes them with the pestle, then pours them into the mortar, where he pounds them into a fine powder: star anise, Szechuan peppercorns, cumin, cardamom, fennel, fenugreek, turmeric, coriander, dried chilis. The aroma is breathtaking and he gathers a bit on his finger and holds it out for me to take a deeper smell.

Vendors sit on the pavement, in the middle of mountains of fresh lemongrass and bunches of long, thin blades of Vietnamese mint, cilantro, curry leaves, turmeric root, galangal, and taro root. There are *chai* carts and samosa carts and carts piled high with Indian sweets, and if someone had blindfolded me and brought me here I would swear I was in the middle of the subcontinent. But I am here, in Singapore, where east meets west and north and south.

In a city proud of its acceptance of western lifestyle and pursuits, and their resultant sterility, here is a pocket of flavour and colour and spice and vivacity. Here is a self-contained, self-ordained mini-country, smaller even than the city-state of Singapore itself, in a symbiotic relationship. Little India feeds off Singapore. It finds its vitality in response to Singapore's lack of below-the-surface lustre.

≈

From Little India I make my way through impersonal tree-lined neighbourhoods to the waterfront, where the lanes are crowded with men in business suits slurping back bowls of noodles or rice or glasses of fresh coconut water. It is lunchtime, and squashed between all the shiny bank towers lined along the shore are Singapore's infamous hawker stalls. They are built into the bases of crumbling colonial buildings and for storeys and storeys above the stalls, the shutters of apartments have been thrown open to the midday sun and the air is littered with laundry, like banners, jutting out from the windows on long thin sticks. The food stall hawkers are shouting out onto the street, letting passers-by know what they are cooking today, what is fresh and good. T-shirts and underwear flutter high overhead.

I have come here with a specific purpose in mind: to try *laksa lemak*. *Laksa* generally refers to any curried noodle dish, but I have heard that Singapore's is the best, the creamiest and most pungent of all *laksas*. It is a classic example of the convergence of cuisines; its Thai influence shows in the use of lemongrass, coconut milk, chilis, the Indian influence in the use of curry, the Chinese influence in the use of rice flour noodles. The Singaporeans add their own touch by throwing in seafood caught in the straits close by, and the Malaysian method for making *rempah* has been appropriated for this dish, as has their penchant for *blachan*, or dried shrimp paste. It is a coming together of five nations in one dish, an appropriate one to be served in expat-ridden, globalized Singapore.

I wander between *laksa* stalls and, not knowing how to differentiate one from the other, I choose the one with the most smiling customers and sit at a stool at a rickety plywood bar. There is no menu. You are here for *laksa lemak* or nothing at all. A heavy, wet breeze blows in from the sea and everyone is limp in the humidity. I stare out at the water and at the freighters and supertankers anchored offshore, far too many to count. Someone told me that off Singapore's coasts there are typically three hundred freighters waiting to load or unload goods and, looking out at them now, that number does not surprise me.

A large bowl is placed in front of me. It is stacked with the freshest of prawns, and squid torsos that have been scored into thousands of little diamond shapes. A few handfuls of bean sprouts teeter on top, and as I lean in to smell it, the screaming yellow broth steams into my nostrils. Divine. Fresh coconut, ocean brine, and a curry so complex it defies dissection (at least in one sitting). The cook hands me a pair of chopsticks and I dive in. The coconut is smooth, but there is something about it that is tart, biting. The seafood is so fresh that I can taste the salt of the waters it swam in this morning. The rice noodles and bean sprouts tame the broth and round out the feel: smooth and spicy and tart, soft and firm and crunchy. Never have I had a dish that accomplished so much in flavour and in texture. A mammoth endeavour, and a masterpiece.

In the next few days, whenever I am tired of Singapore's false-front urbaneness, I return to the street of *laksa* stalls for a dose of life. I try to visit a different one each time, but my palate is not familiar enough with it to be able to tell if one is particularly better than another is. They are all fabulous, and they all make up my best memory of Singapore, which is not one of commerce and boutiques and flashy western clothes. It is of sitting in a small alleyway, slurping curry noodles in the company of finance mucky-mucks who see simplicity and joy in a good bowl of soup just like anyone else, with laundry waving like flags above us between skyscrapers that push into a heavy blue sky and cast shadows on colonial buildings on the shore of a violent green sea.

MALAYSIAN & SINGAPOREAN RECIPES

Roti

To make ghee, or clarified butter, simply melt twice the amount of butter that you will need and skim the milk solids and foam off the top, discarding it. You will be left with a clear yellow liquid. It keeps indefinitely and will solidify at room temperature or in the fridge. Alternatively, you can buy ghee in any east Indian food market.

3 cups white flour
2 eggs
1/2 tsp. salt
3/4 cup warm water
1/2 cup ghee or clarified butter
oil

Place the flour in a large bowl and make a well in the centre. Crack the eggs into the well and sprinkle them with salt. While pouring the water in with one hand, stir the dough with a fork to incorporate the water completely until you have a soft dough. Knead for at least 5 minutes and divide the dough into four pieces. Let the dough rest for at least half an hour and for up to 4 hours. Brush a rolling pin and flat surface with ghee and roll a piece of the dough out until it is paper-thin. Brush the dough with ghee and dust with flour. Roll the dough up like a jellyroll and anchor one end of it. Coil the dough around and on top of the anchored end and press gently down onto it to make a thick round. Repeat with the remaining dough and let the rounds rest for an hour or so. Flour your hands and flatten out a round of the dough to a 6-inch diameter. Grab an edge of the round with the tips of your fingers and fling it out quickly with a snap of the wrist. Move your fingers over slightly and fling again. Keep rotating and flinging until the round is quite thin, and about 12 inches in diameter (alternatively you can use a rolling pin, but flinging is more fun). Bring the edges of the round into the centre of it to make a square. Brush a griddle or large frying pan with ghee and place the roti on it. Cook for 30 seconds, brush the top with more ghee, flip and repeat until both sides of the roti are nicely browned and flaky. Repeat with the remaining rounds and serve immediately. Best eaten straight from the pan.

Serves 4 as part of a meal or as a snack.

Murtabak

This is essentially roti with a filling, in this case, beef. Vietnamese mint, lemongrass, and ghee are available at any Asian or East Indian food market. See the roti recipe for information on ghee.

1 recipe roti dough (see above)
4 shallots, chopped
2 cloves garlic, chopped
1 fresh chili, chopped
1/2 inch fresh ginger, chopped
1/2 tsp. cinnamon
1/4 tsp. ground cloves
1/4 cup Vietnamese mint
1 lemongrass stalk, bottom half only, chopped
2 tbsp. ghee or oil
1/2 lb. ground beef
1/4 cup ghee for frying the *murtabak*

Follow the instructions for the roti and make 4 10-inch rounds of thin dough. Cover them with tea towels and set aside while you make the *rempah*: Pound or grind the shallots, garlic, chili, ginger, cinnamon, cloves, mint, and lemongrass together until you have a paste. Heat 2 tbsp. of the ghee in a wok and add the *rempah*, cooking over medium heat for 8 to 10 minutes. Add the beef, increase the heat to medium-high and cook for a further 4 to 5 minutes, breaking the beef up as it cooks. In the centre of each round, place one-quarter of the beef mixture. Brush the edges of the dough with water and bring them into the centre of the round to make a square. Press the edges together to seal the dough. Brush a griddle or large frying pan with ghee and place the roti on it. Cook for 30 seconds, brush the top with more ghee, flip and repeat until both sides of the roti are nicely browned and flaky. Repeat with the remaining rounds and serve immediately. Best eaten straight from the pan.

Serves 4 as part of a meal or as a snack.

Jagjit's Dalcha

Tamarind, cardamom, and nigella are available at any Asian or East Indian food market.

2 tbsp. tamarind, fresh or pulp

4 cups water

1/2 cup orange lentils

2 cloves garlic, chopped

4 shallots, chopped

2 fresh chilis, chopped

a pinch of cardamom seeds

a pinch of cloves

1/2 tsp. ground turmeric

1/2 tsp. cumin

1 tsp. onion seeds (nigella)

1/2 inch fresh ginger, chopped

1/4 cup ghee, or clarified butter, or oil

2 tomatoes, chopped

1 cup coconut milk

1/2 tsp salt

Soak the tamarind in 1 cup of water for 10 minutes. Scrape the tamarind flesh off the seeds and discard the seeds. Add the tamarind flesh and the water it was soaking in to the remaining water and bring to a boil. Add the lentils and cook over medium-high heat for 20 minutes, until the lentils are soft and have absorbed most of the water. In the meantime, make the *rempah*: Pound or grind the garlic, shallots, chilis, cardamom, cloves, turmeric, cumin, onion seeds, and ginger together to make a paste. Heat the ghee in a wok over medium heat and add the spice paste and tomatoes. Cook for 5 to

6 minutes, until the mixture is fragrant. Add the coconut milk, salt, and cooked lentils. Bring to a boil and cook for 4 to 5 minutes, or until it is as thick as you want it to be (it should be thick enough to be scooped up with a piece of bread or roti). Serve with freshly made roti.

Serves 4 for dinner.

Hawker Stall Laksa

Singapore's most famous street food! Rice noodles, galangal, *blachan*, candlenuts, lemongrass, lime leaves, fish sauce, and Vietnamese mint are available at any Asian market.

1/2 lb. rice noodles
4 shallots, chopped
2 cloves garlic, chopped
1 inch fresh galangal, chopped
1 tsp. dried shrimp paste *(blachan)*
2 fresh chilis, chopped
6 candlenuts or macadamia nuts, chopped
2 tsp. ground turmeric
1 lemongrass stalk, bottom half only, chopped
2 tbsp. oil
4 cups fish stock or water
4 cups coconut milk
2 kaffir lime leaves
12 fresh prawns, peeled
1 tbsp. fish sauce
1 tsp. sugar
salt, to taste
1/2 lb. bean sprouts

2 tbsp. cilantro leaves

2 tbsp. Vietnamese mint, chopped

Pour boiling water over the noodles and let sit until softened, about 2 minutes. Drain and rinse under cold water and set aside. Make the *rempah*: Pound or grind the shallots, garlic, galangal, shrimp paste, chilis, nuts, turmeric, and lemongrass together to make a paste. Heat the oil in a large wok or pot and fry the paste over high heat until it becomes thick and fragrant, about 5 minutes. Reduce the heat to medium and add the stock, coconut milk, and lime leaves and bring to a boil. Cook for 8 to 10 minutes, until it has thickened slightly. Add the prawns and cook for 2 to 3 minutes, until the prawns have just turned pink. Turn off the heat and season with fish sauce, sugar, and salt. Divide the noodles into 4 bowls. Pour the soup over top and garnish with lots of bean sprouts, cilantro and chopped mint.

Serves 4 for dinner.

PATAGONIA

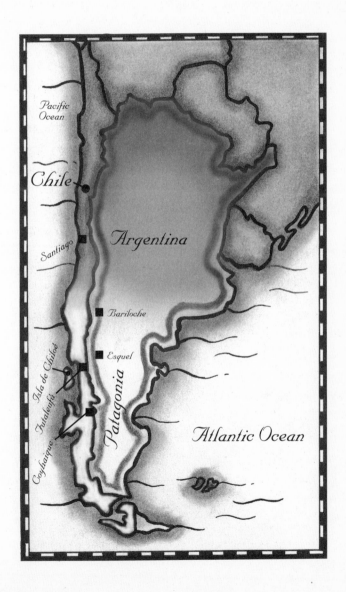

'Patagonia,' he cried. 'She is a hard mistress. She casts her spell. An enchantress! She folds you in her arms and never lets go.' — Bruce Chatwin, In Patagonia

Patagonia is indefinable in most ways. Its boundaries are nebulous; some say it includes the very southern tip of South America that we know as Tierra del Fuego. Others say it doesn't. Everyone agrees that it encompasses states in both southern Chile and southern Argentina, and some are specific enough to say that it lies south of the Rio Negro, but never, ever, in Patagonia do you see evidence that this is definitely where you are. There is no flashing neon sign welcoming you to one of the most remote places on the planet; there is no state, no town, no building that bears its name. Nor will you hear the few people who live there ever mention its name or refer to themselves as Patagonian. But I can tell you with absolute certainty that I was there, alone, on my bike, because what surrounded me could not have been anything but Patagonia.

Patagonia is a mysterious place. It is also quite simply the most beautiful place I have ever been. Friends laughed when I told them I was going there, half out of not knowing exactly where Patagonia was, half out of not knowing why I would possibly want to go there. The truth was, I'd wanted to go there since I could read, and the truth is I have not stopped thinking about it since I got back, and that's going on five years now. Not a day goes by when I don't wish I were there.

It has a landscape and emotion reserved for itself, an aura that is present in no other part of the world. In the vast, unpopulated dry valleys of Argentina and in the clouds above the fjords of Chile, I learned to believe in ghosts. Patagonia is the place where I learned about true desolation and loneliness. And yet it is the same place that taught me more about persona than anywhere else.

Everywhere I went in Patagonia, I heard music: tinny, staticky, blasting out of transistor speakers, old gramophones crackling away. On the main street of a village where the power had suddenly gone out, a truck drove slowly up and down past the houses with a megaphone held out of one of its windows, blaring salsa to lend comfort and to help pass the time. In Santiago, with all the noise in the world around me, a man with a transistor radio dangling from his wrist approached me as I was waiting for something to be fixed. When he found out I was a foreigner, he sat with me for an hour, turning the dial on his radio back and forth trying to find as many different types of Latino music for me to listen to as he could.

There were ghetto blasters on the train heading south towards the Patagonian frontier. When they fell quiet at midnight, a man sitting next to me sang softly in the darkness until it was light again. His fellow travellers woke with smiles on their faces and shook his hand; without him, they would have had to endure silence for a whole evening and that, for Chileans, is as unbearable as the loneliness of their landscape.

On the first morning of my journey into Patagonia, I rode past teenagers stumbling home from a discotheque in the middle of a field that still pumped music through the air. A few days later, sleeping by a lava flow a couple of hours from any sort of settlement, I was woken at one in the morning by a loud tango that played from somewhere close by for exactly one hour and then abruptly stopped, leaving only wind to fill my ears. When I woke in the morning, I looked around at the barren landscape and abandoned road and wondered if I had been hallucinating.

For a while the pervasiveness of the music baffled me, but now it makes perfect sense. The songs alleviated the weight of isolation cascading from Patagonia's vast landscape. They were a reminder of vitality in a part of the world where almost no one lives.

⁀

The first person I meet in Patagonia is a middle-aged Chilean cartographer. I am about 800 kilometres south of Santiago, wandering around under a cloud-covered volcano. When I see him he is seated in the heather halfway up the volcano's flank, staring out at the flow of hardened lava spread across the plain below him. I look up again a moment later and he turns his head towards me, stands, and waves. I pick my way over the lava and sit down beside him. He shakes my hand in silence and, without saying a word, we watch a strong breeze blow over the plain, clouds sink and rinse. For half an hour we listen to the wind ebb and flow over us, and then he stands, shakes my hand again, and walks back down onto the plain. I stay, absorbed in my first glimpse of Patagonia, absorbed in the same vastness and silence that Darwin saw more than 150 years before. The man begins to whistle as he walks down the volcano and his notes drift up to me capriciously, like a feather caught between an updraft and a downdraft, altered by an unseen yet powerful force.

A couple of hours later, while riding through a village I hear his whistle again. He is seated at a roadside café, waving. He raises his coffee cup, waggles it, and shouts "¡Ey! ¡¿ Tomas un café?!" After introducing himself… his name is Enrique… he apologizes for not having spoken on the volcano but, he says, "this was not a place for words to be spoken." I laugh and tell him that I enjoyed the silence. He smiles. "Here is okay. Now we can talk, and you can tell me why you are here," he says.

I tell him that I've wanted to come here for as long as I can remember, that I've forgotten why but that I suspect it has something to do with space. He raises his eyebrows and grins. "¿De veras?" he asks. "Really," I reply. He chuckles and orders another coffee.

Enrique tells me that he works for the national parks of Central and South America and that he comes to this village on weekends to draw people's portraits because he loves to be here. I ask him if he is married and he shakes his head. "No…" He tilts his head pensively as if suddenly wondering why. "No," he says, looking directly at me. "¿Y tú? What does your boyfriend think of this?" he asks, nodding slowly at my bike.

I shrug. "*Estoy sola.*"

"But what does your father think then?"

I shrug again. "*No importa.*"

He throws his head back and laughs. "*¡Bien, bien!*" he shouts, through tears that have suddenly sprung into mirthful eyes. He catches his breath and chuckles. "*¿No tienes novio?*"

"No, no boyfriend."

"I was in *Norteamérica* once," he says. "I saw how the men and women interact. It was," he pauses again, "lacking passion. *Mucha culpa.* Too much guilt." He throws up his hands. "*¿Y por qué?* From where does this come? You are not so religious as we are, but there is this guilt," he leans towards me, making a face and curling his fingers into claws, "hanging over you." "So!" he says triumphantly, "I will give you this piece of advice." He whispers. "*¿Que será? Será.* I think you know this. Things happen over which we have no control. But in order for these things to affect us, we must leave ourselves open and vulnerable, and in order for these things to affect us in a wonderful way, there cannot be any guilt. It is destructive. *¡Inútil!* Useless! *Completamente.*" He takes a sip of his coffee, sits back and thinks. "But it is very difficult to find a person who is like this or even who understands this—a wife, a husband, *un novio, sabes?*"

"*Sí. Yo sé.* But that shouldn't stop you from doing what you want to do."

"*No, no, absolutamente no,*" he says, "but it does. We are too often told that being alone is a bad thing, so we wait around for that person who understands to accompany us, and it doesn't happen and we settle for someone else and feel guilty about it."

"Sí."

"There it is. Guilt again! Forget it! It's better to be alone and if someone comes along, they will find you. ¿Comprendes? ¡Sí!" He throws his fists up in the air and shakes them.

He will not let me pay for the coffee. He writes his cellphone number in my journal. "In case you get into trouble," he says, though we both know I probably won't need it. He walks me over to my bike, shakes my hand, and gives me a kiss on the forehead. He leans towards me, gives my shoulders a shake, and says, "You know, I've been going to that mountain every weekend for twenty years, and no one has ever found me there. Nunca. Except you." He grins, squeezes my hands and walks away.

~

I spend a week negotiating the steep green mountains of Chile, moving up and over their slopes. I pass through villages that are constructed entirely of weathered wood and corrals, where cowboys are busy harnessing cattle. I ride alongside lakes that remind me of fingers, stretching beyond reach into narrow, thin valleys, where men in rowboats wave to me and shout, asking what time it is. At the continental divide, I board an almost empty car ferry that will take me into Argentina. The boat chugs silently through icy alpine waters.

I stand at the bow of the boat, staring into the water. A horn honks and two Argentine men in their thirties beckon me over to their truck. They sit on the tailgate, pouring some dried leaves into a small gourd, covering them with hot water. Carlos places a straw made of silver into the leaves and slurps the water through it quickly. Silvio pours more water on top and motions for me to have a go.

A wave of hot bitter liquid hits my throat. My tongue curls and I try not to squint because I like the flavour. Silvio watches me.

"*¿Azúcar?*" he asks, dropping a sugar cube into the gourd and motioning for me to stir with the straw. I sip. Better. I hand the gourd back.

This is the South American ritual of *yerba mate*. Drunk incessantly throughout the day anywhere south of the Tropic of Capricorn, it is a mild, legal narcotic from the *Ilex paraguaiensis* tree. You can feel its spirit running through your blood while you drink it; initially it produces that same nervous excitement of the first days of being in love, which probably explains why it is so addictive and drunk with such fervour. An hour later you are more relaxed than you have ever been in your life, and with an immensely clear head you realize that you are ravenous.

I am at the prow of the boat, enjoying Patagonia's green peaks and black water when that hunger hits. From the deck above, Silvio shouts "¡Ey!¡Ey! Anik! You want to have eat with us?" How can I turn him down? I join them at their truck again.

We eat tinned paté and cookies and talk. Carlos and Silvio have been kayaking in Chile for the past two weeks—their last trip alone together, says Silvio, because both of their wives are eight months pregnant. "We are so inseparable," he says, slapping Carlos's leg, "that our wives said, okay, we should have children at the same time so that they can be together too." Carlos grins and says their next trip will be with screaming babies in tow. Silvio's eyes widen at the thought. He looks up at the kayaks strapped to the roof of the truck. "Okay," he says, after some thought, and shrugs.

They are stunned that I have never had *mate* before today. I tell them I have been in Chile for only a week. "Yes, we know," they say.

"The Chileans," says Carlos, "are uncivilized and impossible! In Argentina, we would have had some *mate* waiting for you at the airport."

"No!" says Silvio, with a very earnest look on his face. "It would have been served on the plane! What airline did you take from North America?"

"LAN-Chile."

They roll their eyes. "And no *mate?*" Carlos jabs Silvio in the ribs. "You see? Uncivilized!"

As the boat docks, they give me a jar of condensed milk thickened into caramel. Carlos tells me to spread it on bread like honey. He points to the name on the label, *manjar*. "*Es Chileno.* In Argentina, we call it '*dulce de leche*' (sweet milk). *Qué nombre! Manjar...* " He shakes his head. I give them a jar of peanut butter in return. "*¡Ay!¡Qué rico!*" he says and holds it up victoriously, shouting at Silvio. "Peanut butter! We can't get this in Argentina! Where did you buy this?" he asks.

I lie. "Santiago," I say, and wink at Silvio.

Carlos's eyes darken. "*Los chilenos!*"

On the Argentine side of Patagonia, the landscape is even more vast than in Chile. Brown and golden valleys run between lines of rocky peaks. It is dry; the sun is blinding and intense. The wind, starting as a crosswind from the west in the mornings, builds to gale-force strength and swings slowly around to meet me head-on each afternoon. I limp southward in low gear through scorched land, large ranches and *estancias* the only sign of life. Occasionally the whistles of *gauchos* herding their cattle drift past me in the wind and I scan the horizon for them, rarely finding them. Uphills are a relief—they are the only place where the wind seems to diminish. I pedal pathetically into Bariloche, a resort town, where a once-proud Argentine flag is being ripped from its pole in an upward stretch by a Patagonian breeze, and where a woman who runs a place where one can make international phone calls asks why I would want to call Canada when it is much cheaper to call Brazil.

I pass deep alpine lakes that lie at the base of sawback ranges. I pedal under an enormous sky, the likes of which I have seen only in Southern Alberta and Montana. The resemblance is so close that I swear to God I am there, not a whole hemisphere away. I am sun-burned, weatherbeaten, hardened, my face etched with the ritual scars of squinting; white lines of crow's-feet splay from the corners of my eyes. I am sweaty, dirty, caked in dust from the gravel roads, bruised from rocks that fly up from my front wheel and from haul-ing a loaded bicycle through cavernous potholes. I am a sight to see.

Halfway up a pass, I am stopped, still straddling the bike, shin-deep in gravel, resting my head and arms on my handlebars. The sun beats down on my salt-encrusted back. I look up and notice a small pick-up truck that has pulled up quietly beside me. Two young men peer out of the windows at me. I smile. "*Hola.*"

They nod and look at each other. "*¿Necesitás socorro?*" they ask. Do I need help? Oh, probably…

"*No. Está bien, gracias.*"

They grin and cut the engine on their truck. The man on the pas-senger side opens his door carefully, steps out, and looks at me, then goes to the back of the truck. He silently pulls out a propane burner and fires it up. He places a tin kettle full of water on the flame and rummages around for some *mate*.

I watch them, still leaning on my handlebars. The driver pulls two lawn chairs out of the back and sets them up in the middle of the road. He motions for me to have a seat. The *mate* is ready. Usually the person making the *mate* takes the first sips from the gourd because they are the most bitter, but the driver takes one look at me and obviously decides to abandon the tradition. He pours the water over the leaves and hands the gourd over to me right away. His friend starts to protest but he waves the words into silence, and they both watch me intently. I empty the gourd in a few sips and they applaud. They introduce themselves: Búby and Fabiano.

We sit in the road and talk for a while—it is a funny scene; two vacationing young butchers from Neuquén and a wrecked cyclist in the middle of what has been dubbed "the worst road in all of

Argentina, period," leaning back in lawn chairs, laughing, sipping *mate*, miles from nowhere. But of course there is no one else to see it.

When the *mate* is finished, Búby and Fabiano wave their hands at the landscape and tell me that this is no place for a woman to be. When I start laughing, their serious looks crumble and they realize that perhaps it doesn't matter. They offer an ultimatum. I can either keep on going and spend the night camped alone by a river, eating stale bread, mushy bananas, and cheese, or I can let them load my bike onto the truck, drive a short distance to El Bolsón, camp with them, and let them cook an *asado*, the traditional and infamous Argentine barbecue.

⌐

An *asado* is not something to be trifled with in Argentina, especially when in the grips of a pair of butchers. The success of an *asado* is generally measured by the length of the grill that the meat is cooked on. I heard a woman once, when asked if her son's wedding went well, reply, "Yes! The *asado* was twenty metres long!" Even though there are just the three of us, Búby and Fabiano set out to make it the most successful one they have ever had. They gather wood for an hour, light it, and blow on its coals delicately. Only when the coals are the exact right colour do they lay the meat over the grill. Beef is a staple in Argentina; in fact, it is useless to try to find anything else to eat. At an *asado*, every part of the cow is put on the grill, the most obscure parts being the most revered. Búby and Fabiano hand me a plate stacked with three or four different cuts of steak, *riñones* (kidneys), *morcilla* (blood sausage), *tripa* (tripe), *ubre* (udder) and *chinchulines* (small intestines). "This," says Búby, pointing to two testicular bulbs sizzling over the fire, "is only for the men." I stagger under the weight of the plate and sit down, waiting for them to join me. Then I notice that they are busy grilling more food and that this massive plate I am holding is entirely my own.

Búby and Fabiano

The flavour is outstanding. Búby slaps the meat on the grill as is, unadulterated. Not even salt. Now, as its juices run over my tongue, I realize what beef is supposed to taste like: somewhat gamey, like it has been alive. Fabiano takes a bite and his eyes light up. He says, "This cow ate sweet grass. Can you taste it?"

They talk about Neuquén and the shop and how they take their vacation together every year. Friendship and family are the backbone of Latino society and, Fabiano says, one can only improve oneself with the help of elders, siblings, and buddies. "I'm not talking about money or a job. I'm talking about one's *alma*, one's soul. You cannot know yourself unless you know your soul." Búby nods and nods. "*¿Por qué viajás sola?*" he asks me.

"It's just my way of doing it. *Mucho tiempo para pensar.* Lots of time to think. And it's difficult to find someone to do it with."

Búby looks at me and pierces a piece of meat with his fork. "It's better with a man. A man who really understands you," he says, waving his fork at me.

I blink slowly, smile, and think of Enrique. "I've been told that before."

⌒

I continue south towards Cholila and Esquel. The landscape becomes drier, vaster. The sun is harsher, the sky a paler blue. There is absolutely no risk of claustrophobia here, no risk of feeling things closing in on you. Cholila is where Butch Cassidy came when America became "too small" for him, and I understand why. It is in this Patagonian landscape that three fugitives in the film *Caballos Salvajes* pull into a gas station and its owner, instead of calling the police and collecting a $15,000 reward, tells the fugitives to wait while he makes them a lunch of warm *milanesas* (steak sandwiches) and wine, and then tells them what roads to take to avoid the police. When you meet the people here, that is just what you would expect them to do. The camaraderie here is necessitated by the isolation of the landscape.

It is a place where I somehow lose my wallet and where a woman insists on driving me slowly up and down a stretch of road where I could have lost it. It is where, at a seemingly abandoned but operational gas station at the intersection of two dirt paths where tumbleweed swirls across empty plains, two young men offer an unsolicited promise to look for it. It is where a policeman standing within earshot has me come back to his one-room station where he stamps out a report on an ailing typewriter, with six carbon copies (for whom? I had just met all four people who lived there). It is a place where, a few days later when the two young men see me again in a town farther down the road, they run up to tell me that they have not yet found my wallet and that they are still looking.

I cross into Chile again near the town of Futaleufú. If I thought I was in Patagonia before, it does not even compare to the Patagonia I am in now. From the open steppes and sandstone-coloured mountains of Argentina, I pass the frontier and enter a cacophony of landscape, of verdant mountains crashing into each other, of snarling vegetation and roaring rivers. There is a quality of sharpness in everything that is unfathomable. Darwin called it "nature's workshop."

I roll into town just after dark and stand in an abandoned plaza in the centre of town. It is dimly lit by strings of lights that swing violently in a sudden breeze, surrounded by the spiky, swooning branches of Patagonia's famous *araucarías*, monkey puzzle trees. I look across the plaza and see a store whose front window is crammed with small wooden ships. The dim light of a candle waivers behind them and the silhouette of a tall thin man fills the door frame. He whistles to get my attention and asks if I need anything. I ask him if there is a place to camp around here.

"Sure," he says, pointing behind me, "down by the river, at the bridge there. There's some good flat ground. And all the water in the world. But why don't you come in for a coffee first?"

The inside of the shop is crammed with more wooden ships— everything is wooden… the walls, the creaky, worn floorboards, coated in a fine sheen of sawdust. Luís clears some old newspapers off a table and beckons me to sit. He brings warm milk and instant coffee and I ask him about the boats. It seems a strange thing to sell in the mountains. He smiles and says, "One is never far from the sea in Chile." This is true. At its greatest breadth, Chile is only 120 kilometres wide.

Luís takes me down to the river and helps me set up my tent. We sit by the water for a while, listening to it rush over rocks. He tells me this is the most beautiful river in Chile and if he could, he would build a house over it so that he would be reminded of its beauty at any given moment. After a long silence, he gets up and bids me goodnight, but returns ten minutes later to find me still sitting there. He smiles and says, "Ah, the Futaleufú, she has you now…. She won't let go." He has brought me a bag of bread and cheese and *mate*, and wishes me a good trip. When he turns to leave, he is immediately absorbed into the darkness.

In the morning, I mount my bicycle and follow the Futaleufú. As the day progresses, the road gets worse and worse. It climbs through green peaks and descends along craggy, rocky banks of water so violent that I can barely hear my wheels crunching on the road. Portions of the road are transformed into deep crevasses by waterfalls that tumble from the mountainsides. The entire day I see only two *gauchos*, who nod curtly and raise a forefinger from their reins as I pass them. With scarcely a farmhouse in sight, the road spirals westward; elbow-jarring gravel bumps me down to a lake where I call it quits for the day, where a string of peaks and glaciers lies at the foot of a warm, azure lake. Three Chileans fly-fishing nearby flash silver tails of line back and forth until the sky turns black.

The Carretera Austral is the only road that heads south from here, a washboarded, potholed path that winds in and out of the mountains, to and from the coast, connecting glaciers and rainforests and glaciers again. The road was Augusto Pinochet's project, intended to open up the isolated south for the Chileans, and it is virtually abandoned; it is much easier to travel by boat in these parts than to navigate the steep mountain passes. The road stretches 650 kilometres south from Puerto Montt and dissolves just beyond the settlement of Coyhaique, where the mess of land and water becomes too complicated to be accessible.

I pass a lonely hitchhiker as I turn onto the Carretera. He seems ready to camp out for a few days waiting for a ride, but waves cheerfully as I ride by. Near the seaside village of Puyuguapi, pigs and chickens are scattered across the Carretera, the only road through town, and I have the feeling that if asked, no one would be able to say where this road goes. Nor would it matter. No one travels alone here, and of the few cars that pass me every day, each driver stops to talk, shattering the isolation and loneliness they feel when they travel through these green fjords. They offer me rides, water, food, directions on a road that is only going one place, a reality check... whatever they can give me that will make my life easier. They always ask, "¿No tienes miedo?" Aren't you scared? they say, with wide eyes searching around them as if something horrible could happen to us here, in the presence of nothing but land, sea, and sky.

By an inlet, I pause to watch four men try to get a full-grown cow into a rowboat. Imagine that. At sunset, as I'm pedalling alongside the ocean, I hear a splash and look beside me. A porpoise hovers in the water, staring curiously at me. For the next hour, she follows me, dives in and out of the water beside me, watching my pedals turn until the road heads inland again. I camp on the side of the road, about halfway up a pass, clouds hovering a foot over my head. Here I am able to put a finger on the feeling of this place. The isolation is so pervasive and the solitude so complete that I don't trust it. I know that I am always being watched by something, someone. I fall asleep to the sound of owls hooting in the forest behind me.

I wake with a start in the middle of the night. The wind is pushing through the pass, whistling through stunted trees. In the background I swear I can hear someone, a human, breathing. The breathing rotates around my tent for an hour or so, occasionally fading out, but coming back with the regularity of my own breath. I keep drifting in and out of sleep, too tired to stick my head out and investigate. I wake again, this time fully. I lie stock-still, not knowing what has yanked me from my fitful dreams. Suddenly a howling begins, first on my right, about three feet away, then my left, then at my feet and suddenly all around. Like the howls of coyotes, but higher in pitch, each howl is an intricate series of notes, so close I can hear the howlers, in a ring around my tent, pause for breath. Just before dawn the howls fade and I sleep again for an hour. I sit up, open my vestibule, and rub my eyes awake. In front of me, between the fly and the tent, is a stack of bread in a dish towel, still warm, from some invisible household on this stretch of road full of the ghosts of Patagonia. I wonder how much of what happened last night was imagined in my exhaustion. And then I unzip the fly, look at the green mountains tumbling into one another, with ice in all their nooks and crannies, and I realize that none of it was imagined at all. That this is where spirits live. That there are no words to describe it.

I have the road all to myself today. Not a single car, horse, or motorbike passes. Towards the end of the day, I pass a farmstead with a single white flag hung by the road… a sign in rural Chile for a place that sells home-made bread. I leave the bike by the road and walk up to a farmhouse that has bursts of smoke puffing out of a tin chimney. I knock on the door, and when a little girl answers I ask if she still has some bread left. She looks at me with large brown eyes, then nods slowly. Her grandmother appears and waves me into her kitchen, where she is kneading dough in a shallow open box with three sides. She takes a piece of wood and throws it into an airtight stove. The little girl hops up onto a stool by the stove and grasps a big wooden spoon. She places it in a large pot that sits over the fire and stirs unsteadily. Her grandmother grins at me and points a waggly finger at the pot. "*Leche*," she says, "*en dos horas, manjar.*" She fills a bag with little pucks of bread still warm to the touch, pats me on the arm, and asks, "Are you the girl on the bike? From Canada?" I pause, narrow my eyes, and look at her for a moment before answering. "*Sí*," I say cautiously. She grins, pats me on the arm again, and says, "Está bien, está bien." She dips her head at me when I say goodbye, and they watch me walk down the path back to the road, giving me a quick wave just before I go out of sight. I now understand the magic realism of South American stories, and wish I could live in a place where it exists.

The next day, at the end of the Patagonian road for me, I sit in Coyhaique's central square, cooling down from the ride into town. An old man standing on the edge of the square sees me and approaches. He asks me where I came from on my bike. Argentina, I tell him. He stares at my bike for a while and then at me. "Has it been a good time for thinking?" he asks. I smile. He smiles back, and wanders off, clutching a book behind his back with both hands, staring up at the sky as if it is something new, something to be noticed. I follow his gaze, and when the sun glints off the corner of a thick white cloud, I know that this is the first time I have seen a sky too.

To finish the trip, I take a ferry up the coast to the island of Chiloé, a place where witches still exist and where life is simply simple. The boat passes through narrows of volcanoes and snow-capped peaks lit by a full moon. I sleep outside on the deck so I can catch a last glimpse of Patagonia, and at three in the morning, someone sees me awake and offers me some mate. He sits down beside me and as he passes the gourd, he tells me about his life. He is an engineer from Temuco, in central Chile, who has taken a few weeks off to see the south for the first time in his life; on his way back up to Temuco, he will visit his family. They live by the sea in a small town on Chiloé, and there will be a celebration tonight when he arrives. "Because you're coming home?" I ask. Hernán shrugs and shakes his head. "No, just because… "

He tells me there will be wine and curanto, a famous Chilote dish served at fiestas, then nudges me and says, "You should come! I will teach you how to make *curanto*, and how to dance the *cueca*. My mother would be thrilled to have an interested guest."

And indeed she is. When we arrive, she takes my face into her hands and kisses it fiercely, slaps me on the shoulders several times, and drags me into the house to show me how far along the party preparations are. The house is jammed with people—it is a house typical of those found on rainy Chiloé—it has one large main room that was the original building, but with each new addition to the family, a new room was tacked on so that now the house looks like a pile of wooden cubes stacked by a child, ready to topple into the sea.

Hernán takes me out to the back, where the *curanto* is being prepared. A large pit has been dug and a fire lit the day before. Rocks are placed around the fire, and when the fire dies, some wet seaweed is spread over the rocks, the combination creates a flavourful steam, cooking and permeating the food that is placed on top of it. Three men stand by the pit, wrapping chicken, sausage, potato dumplings, and masses and masses of mussels, seabass, prawns, and clams in large leaves, placing them on top of the seaweed. More hot stones are placed on top, and the whole thing is left to cook. "For how long?" I ask. One of the men looks at me for a long while, tilts his head, and smiles. "Until it is done," he says.

Hernán and I walk down to the water and stand among the *palafitos*, the stilted houses of the village, taking in a tremendous view. A storm is coming, and the mountains on the mainland are yellow, streaked in sunshine. The ocean glimmers with reflection, and an unsettling wind bursts around us. Some villagers are gathering seaweed to dry on the asphalt of the roads, and as we watch them, I ask Hernán what his impression of the Chilean people is. He sighs and says, "You know, I had to live away from Chile for seven years to figure that out. We are a strong people, *muy fuerte*, but strong in silence, eh?" He looks at me to make sure I understand what he means. "How come no one talks about Pinochet?" I ask. He looks over at the mainland and is quiet. After a while, shrugs and says with a sigh, "When you endure something like that and it is finished, you do not want to talk about it any more. You have given it enough of your time." He pauses. "And if you give it any more, it might just kill you."

We move back to the house, where the party is in full swing. In the living room, all the furniture has been cleared and everyone is packed into the room. There are three guitar players, and we all clap in time as they belt out their songs. Half a dozen men in the centre of the room, dressed in their best duds, stamp out their *cueca*, expertly waving white handkerchiefs, surrendering to the women, who flit coyly about in swishy dresses, purposely avoiding their suitors. The dance is based on the mating rituals between the rooster and hen, and when a man and woman get close to each other, the whole crowd whistles shrilly and cheers, the clapping increases dramatically, and everyone grins as wildly as is possible.

The *curanto* comes in bits and pieces from outside. When I go out to the pit to help, I see an amazing transformation in the sky has occurred. A black swath of cloud hangs inches overhead and the ocean has turned grey and frothing. The mainland has disappeared completely behind a low bank of fog; Chiloé's hills are lustrous, seductive, teasing the rain that is about to fall from the sky. They are a shade of green so deep that I feel enveloped by it. Hernán stands beside me, smiling and nodding. "*Chile*," he says quietly and then looks at me. "*Esto es Chile*."

And at the end of the evening, with all the wine finished, the *curanto* devoured, the dancing done, and everyone collapsed around the table, I look at Hernán's family and cannot imagine a set of people I would be more likely to call my friends. I feel as though

Chile has found me alone in a very dark tunnel, and that in all the darkness, the smallest ray of sunshine has appeared far in the distance, attached itself to me as an imaginary rope, and slowly drawn me out into its pure and unadulterated light.

PATAGONIAN RECIPES

Mate

The ultimate ice-breaker in South America, sharing *mate* is an experience not to be turned down, least of all because it is considered rude to refuse an offer of it. While it is an acquired taste, the ritual of its service and the access that it affords you into people's everyday lives will help you overcome its initial bitter taste. *Yerba mate* is available in any Latin America food store, as are the gourds and *bombillas*, or straws that one sucks the liquid through.

Fill the *mate* gourd three-quarters full with *yerba mate*. Heat some water and just before it boils (do not let it boil or the *mate* will be ruined!) place the *bombilla* in the gourd and slowly pour the water next to the straw, until the gourd is full.

The person serving the *mate* drinks the first cup, then refills it with water and hands it to the next person, clockwise. It is considered uncouth to drink the *mate* slowly, or to hand back a gourd with water still in it. Drink all of it, and if you want more, slurp with the straw when you have finished, and the server will remember you on the next round. If you don't want more, simply say *gracias*. Never refill the gourd yourself—always let the server do it. Being offered *mate* is a form of acceptance. Relish it!

Manjar or Dulce de Leche

In Patagonia, manjar or dulce de leche is used like honey. Chileans and
Argentines spread it on biscuits, bread, sponge cake, or cookies, or pour it on top of fresh fruit.

8 cups whole milk (3.25% B.F. or higher)
2 cups sugar
½ tsp. vanilla
1 tsp. baking soda

Bring the milk to a boil over high heat, then reduce the heat
to medium and remove the skin that has formed on top.
Repeat the process two or three more times, until the skin
that forms is very thin. Add the sugar and vanilla to the milk,
stir for 2 minutes until it is dissolved, and simmer over medium heat. Add the baking soda and cook for 2 minutes, then
skim the foam off with a spoon. Cook the milk for 2 hours,
stirring and skimming occasionally. Be careful not to stir the
skin that has formed on the sides of the pot into the milk
mixture, as this will cause the milk to curdle and the sugar to
crystallize. The milk will thicken and darken, and should be
stirred more often the darker it gets. A crust will likely have
formed on the bottom of the pot, but do not disturb this
when you stir. Cook the milk until it is a caramel colour, then
pour it through a fine strainer and let it cool. The manjar will
thicken further on cooling and will keep in the refrigerator
indefinitely.
Makes 2 cups.

Asado

The quintessential Argentine experience, this barbeque is prepared in a very specific way. Use a wood fire, not a propane barbecue, and never, ever use lighter fluid or charcoal, which alter the flavour of the meat. A hibachi is the perfect thing to use for an *asado* for two people. After the initial fire has turned into embers, feed it occasionally with more wood. The meat will take longer to cook than on a regular barbecue, but will be much more flavourful. All the meats below are available at a good butcher's.

1 lb. wood per person, lit with newspaper and
    allowed to burn into embers
6 chorizo sausages
2 morcillas or blood sausages
6 beef kidneys, left whole
2 lb. tripe, left whole
6 sweetbreads, cleaned and left whole
5 lb. rib eye steaks
2 lb. flank steak

Place the meats that will take the longest to cook on the fire first (all of these listed should take about the same time, depending on the thickness of the steaks). Cook until tender, turning the meats the traditional four times. Place a little bit of everything on each plate and serve plain, or with a good loaf of bread and some chimichurri sauce on the side.
Serves 6 for dinner.

Chimichurri sauce

This is Argentina's answer to salsa, served with grilled meat.

2 small onions, chopped
1 green pepper, chopped
2 small green chili peppers, chopped
3 tomatoes, chopped
a bunch of parsley, chopped
6 tbsp. vinegar
6 tbsp. oil
3 cloves garlic, chopped
a bunch of cilantro, chopped
½ tsp. salt
¼ tsp. pepper

Combine all the ingredients in a bowl
and let sit for an hour or so, to let the
flavours blend.

Serves 6 as a condiment.

THAILAND

Countries live in people.
—Karen Connelly, *Dream of a Thousand Lives: A Sojourn in Thailand*

It seems that everyone I know who has been to Bangkok has arrived
at midnight, when sheer exhaustion and darkness heighten the senses
and make arrival in a new world surreal. Those friends recount
with startling clarity the first wave of heat and humidity; the first
wave of ceaseless noise, horns honking, the constant roar of muffler-
less traffic, the shouts of street vendors over bustling motorcades, the
shrieking whistles of traffic police in constant arpeggio; the first
wave of the scent of human sewage lingering beneath the smell of
charcoal, charred meat, rotting fish, the perfume of a fermented fruit
they could not identify. Smiles creep unaware across their faces as
they remember being shocked by what they heard and saw and felt,
but understand without a doubt that Bangkok was part of a profound, character-forming moment that changed them forever.

If you want to know yourself as a traveller, Southeast Asia is an
important place to be. By important, I mean of great import on the
larger scale of things, as weighty as the culture of Europe, or the
sheer experience of Africa, or the sensuous inundation of India, all
of which show us how far we have come as a species, in intellect, in
endurance, in utility, and in mere survival. Southeast Asia has a way
of redefining things. The common misconception is that it makes
you appreciate the "privilege" of being born into a western country
and its potential for affluence. In fact, what Southeast Asia does is
reveal the excesses of the West, of how we westerners have lost sight

of the importance of simpler things in the quest for money and "meaningful" careers (as opposed to a meaningful existence), the need for a house or two or three, a car or two or three, and material possessions. Southeast Asia has a way of forcing you to define what is absolutely necessary for your survival and uncover the happiness that lies within a possessionless existence.

⌇

I step out of the airport at 1 a.m. local time and walk into a wall of noise and humidity so dense it suppresses thought. I stand on a sidewalk, sweat already running in rivulets over my skin. I gaze in awe at a massive tangle of automobiles charging down a highway at breakneck speed. I hear only engines. Millions of them, all at once, all in front of me.

I join a long queue of Thais waiting to dash across six lanes of expressway to get to the public bus stop. At the first small blip in traffic, a tiny woman beside me grabs my hand and pulls me across the pavement in a frantic trot, dodging speeding cars and three-wheeled tuk-tuks. She emits a long, loud shriek as we run, gasping with relief when we make it to the other side. The people waiting for the bus smile and laugh at us and slap us on our backs. They chat among one another as bus after bus careens past at full speed. For half an hour we stand on a small strip of raised pavement that separates two lines of cacophonous, rapidly moving traffic. A bus finally stops and after a brief chat with the driver, I am pushed to the front of the line where everyone motions for me to get on. The woman who hauled me across the highway presses a note written in Thai into my hand and tells me to show it to the driver. A man standing with us takes my arm and gets on the bus with me, indicating to the others that he'll make sure I get to where I'm going (which even I am unsure of). I pay my ten-cent fare and watch the others on the platform leaning out into the traffic, searching for the next bus.

For the next two hours, the bus trundles along the main thoroughfares of Bangkok, passing countless makeshift slums built beneath overpasses, beside factories, in concrete public squares, next to heavily fenced homes and armoured guards. Wherever there is light, there are throngs of people, standing, walking, eating steaming food at stalls, strolling, resting, prone on the sidewalk, sleeping. The bus seldom stops. The man who got on with me occasionally points at things for me to look at—elaborate golden temple roofs hidden behind whitewashed walls, a gigantic frangipani tree in violent bloom, with petals dripping from its stems. He drifts in and out of sleep for a while, then wakes, pats my leg, and tells me I should get off here.

And so, at 4 a.m., jet-lagged, grimy with sweat and soot, completely lost but not caring, I stand at an unknown intersection in the middle of Bangkok and look around at this crazy, chaotic place on a continent I have never been to before and grin. I stand drenched in noise and humidity and plumes of all scents possible, thinking, "Jesus H. Christ… "

I choose a direction and walk down a narrow road that leads away from the intersection. It is lined with brightly painted food carts, each lit with a string of lights or a propane lantern, steam and aroma breaking over my nose as I pass them. The carts are crowded with customers shovelling rice or noodles efficiently into their mouths, carrying on discussions in abrupt, clacking tones. The hiss and sizzle of woks and deep-fryers drown out the traffic in the distance and for a moment I forget that I am in the middle of one of the largest cities in Asia. I would have thought it more likely to find this small road and the smiling faces on it in a rural settlement, the only noises those of oil spitting, the clanging of metal spoons on woks, and tongues busy with words, slurping, laughing.

A customer at one of the carts whistles and waves me over. He points to the wok, silently asking if I'd like something to eat. He touches his bottom eyelid gently a few times, telling me that it will make me feel less tired. The cart owner peers at me from under a large, conical straw hat, then, grinning, he grabs a piece of meat and places it on a chopping board so worn into concavity it could be used as a bowl. In a rapid staccato of metal on wood, he attacks the meat with two cleavers, mincing it in a matter of seconds. After he pours a bit of oil into the wok, he stirs it with a pair of chopsticks and with his other hand tosses in a constant stream of ingredients— garlic, chilis, shallots, lemongrass, chopped coriander and its root, the minced beef. A sharp, spicy smell hits my nose and drifts around me. Deftly, he adds some liquid, a bit of sugar, then lines a large plastic bowl with lettuce leaves. He spoons the beef into it and pushes it towards me, smiling, showing me how to take one of the lettuce leaves and fold it so it is sturdy enough to use as a spoon. Someone else has brought me a small plastic bag that reminds me of the ones goldfish come in, but this bag is bulging with a clear brown liquid and translucent lumps. It is a drink called grass jelly. A straw is stuck into the knot that seals the bag, and a few people in the crowd that has now gathered show me how to loop my baby finger through the knot and let the drink dangle from my hand as a way of holding it. The beverage is slightly sweet and very refreshing, slipping down my throat in bumps and slides. Once I start eating, the crowd dissipates.

I have heard that Bangkok governments are forever trying to outlaw street vending, using the excuse of reducing congestion. With my tongue trembling from the collision of flavours in this dish, which the cart owner calls *neua pad keemao*, I can only assume that the officials in charge of these pursuits do not indulge in the streetside gastronomy in their own city. The owner of the cart speaks to me in English and tells me that I have already learned the most important rule of assimilation in Thailand: snacking. Thais do not sit down to a large meal with any regularity, he says. "We have curious palates, and the best way to satisfy a curious palate is to have a little bit of this, a little bit of that, all the time."

When I finish, the owner smiles and bows slightly in the Thai *wai*, which is a way of expressing all sorts of things: thank you, you're welcome, pleased to meet you—it is a sign of respect, and a way of shaking hands. I *wai* back and he laughs. When I shove my hands in my pockets, I feel the piece of paper the woman at the airport gave me. I pull it out and show it to him. He nods, and looks around. He shouts to a young boy sitting nearby, then hands him the piece of paper and points to me. He pats the boy on the shoulder and pushes us down the street with a smile.

The boy is quiet and walks in front of me, dipping down *sois*, or alleyways, walking past ramshackle houses built anywhere there is space, each house with a light on and some sort of perfumy scent reminiscent of incense drifting from it. For twenty minutes we walk through narrow *sois* stained with large puddles of motor oil and radiator fluid, past caged storefronts with a view of families sleeping on the floor inside. We pass a man selling sticky rice wrapped in pyramids of pandan leaves from two large wicker baskets slung across his shoulders by a bamboo yoke. I buy two and give them to the boy because he'll probably have a long walk home. He smiles and tells me his name. Phat eats the rice delicately, slowing his pace so that now he walks beside me. Dawn creeps into the sky.

We come to the end of a claustrophobic alley, houses teetering above and threatening to fall on top of us. The alley is dirt, potholed and bumpy, and behind us, someone is opening shop. A large metal door slides open to reveal a room full of auto grease and rubber. A mechanic in coveralls walks out, looks up and down the alley, and re-enters his shop. Phat stops in front of a large house and points at it. Behind it is a *klong*, one of Bangkok's many canals, where long thin boats full of forty or fifty people skim past. Phat grabs my wrist and pulls me into the open doorway of the house. When we call out, a woman emerges from behind a curtain. She *wais*, we *wai*, and she reads the note Phat gives her. As she sees that I'm not entirely sure what the note says, she grins. Patting my arm, she tells me that the person who gave me the note is her friend, that I can rent a room if I like.

The sun sears itself to the eastern horizon in a huge, red ball. I am not tired at all—the man at the food stall was right—so after dropping my bag in my room, I go out to wander in the *sois* some more. The traffic—pedestrian, bicycle, motorized—has increased in the *sois*, and out on the main streets it has already become the snarl that it will remain for the rest of the day.

After a couple of hours of walking beside the *klongs* (which are almost as snarled as the streets), I am hungry again. I go into a restaurant with three seats and ask if they have some breakfast. The chef, a fourteen-year-old girl wearing a Chanel Paris T-shirt, Birkenstocks, and a black plastic bag for an apron, motions for me to sit.

The alleyway I'm in is littered with laundry, rattan baskets at least four feet high, kids, a Coca-Cola umbrella, a hibachi, flat tires, motorcycle parts, and coconut husks. A man pulls up on a scooter laden with three large baskets. He tips one of them over in front of the kids and a large pile of guava, durian, and pineapple tumbles out. The kids scoop the fruits off the ground and bring them to the chef. Within seconds I have a plate of fresh fruit in front of me. A few minutes later, the chef brings out a large pot of soupy rice called *khao tom* and several bowls, filled with dried shrimp, *nam pla prik* (a ubiquitous fish sauce-based condiment), deep fried shallots, minced roasted peanuts, coriander, and large-leaved purple basil. She calls the kids over, service grinds to a halt, and we settle in, decorating small bowls of the rice soup with the condiments, then spooning the gruel into our mouths and letting the flavours swim and simmer in saliva.

As we eat, a shiny new Mercedes pushes through the alley, through the plastic and the garbage and over a pair of abandoned, dilapidated thongs. Its driver is talking on a mobile phone. The roar of boat engines in the klong behind us drowns out any conversation we might have.

～

I somehow find my way back to the house where I am renting a room, and when I knock on the door, Andaman opens it and giggles, telling me that it is always unlocked and that I should just walk in. Carrying a bowl of fresh frangipani flowers floating in water, she follows me up to my room. She asks me questions about my family and Canada, wants to know what I do and why I'm not doing it now. When she asks me about food in Canada, I laugh. I tell her I think it is a little dull, richer than it is flavoured, and that we are only just starting to embrace spice. She holds her hand out. "Come, I show you how to make something for your friends." Taking her hand, I follow her down into a tiny kitchen crammed with pots and strainers and bamboo baskets.

Andaman brings out a stool and pushes me down onto it. She puts a large clay mortar and wooden pestle in my hands. Into the mortar she places a purple-tinted clove of garlic, a few pinches of salt, a couple of tiny bird chilis, and a handful of roasted peanuts. She rummages around under her open sink and emerges with a large bottle. She lets me inhale its pungent odour. "Fish sauce. Very good." Placing her thumb over its lip, she shakes some of it into the mortar. She squeezes in the juice of a lime and sprinkles some palm sugar and dried shrimp over top. Moving behind me, she wraps her arms around me and grabs my forearms, showing me how to pound everything into a paste with the pestle. Satisfied with my movement, she stands back and looks pleased. At the back of the kitchen, she opens a rickety door. The edge of the house teeters over a klong and Andaman leans out her door, looking up and down the waterway. She whistles sharply, shouts something, and beckons for me to bring her a little jar of coins that sits on the table.

She has hailed a long, narrow wooden boat. Its owner sits in the back and places her thin paddle along the length of her vessel. In front of her splayed in large, beautiful baskets is a tremendous array of fruit: finger bananas, pineapples, durian, fuzzy rambutans, heaps of lychees and longans, green papayas. Their mix of scents drifts up to me, and Andaman smiles at the look of excitement on my face. She says something in Thai to the vendor and points to a gorgeous, long, green papaya. Without so much as wobbling the boat, the vendor leans forward, grabs it, places it on a scale in front of her, and barks a price up to Andaman. Andaman hands her some coins. The vendor passes up the papaya, smiles at me, *wais*, and pushes herself away from the canal wall. I watch her as she paddles her flat-bottomed boat full of fruit serenely down the canal—a woman in a large straw hat selling her wares on the water.

Inside, Andaman attacks the green papaya, which is the size of a small watermelon. She deftly peels it, leaving it whole, then quickly makes deep cuts into it with an enormous cleaver while I keep pounding the paste. She shaves long, thin strips off the papaya and the whole thing collapses into a pile of julienned strips. She throws a small handful into the mortar as I pound, looks at my work, nods briskly, and says, "Good." She chops a tomato or two, throws that in, and watches me bash everything together for another minute or so. Heaping the remaining papaya into the mortar, she tells me to pound it gently until everything is mixed together.

She lines a plate with lettuce leaves, then finally takes the mortar from my hands and dumps the papaya mixture on top. She holds the plate out to me. "*Som tam*," she says, pointing to it. "Very important in Thailand."

I lean over and smell it. In one sniff exists all the flavours detectable by the palate: sweet, sour, salty, bitter. I take a bite. The papaya meanders around my mouth. The fish sauce imparts a pungent flavour reminiscent of fermented grapes and anchovies, but smooths everything out at the same time. My mouth is full of so many flavours that I don't want to swallow, so I just move everything about with my tongue for a few moments until it has stretched its feelers out wide, as if waking for the first time in its life. Andaman watches me and laughs and laughs and laughs.

⋲

In the late afternoon, I am in the kitchen of Andaman's house, chatting about nothing in particular, learning Thai words. Andaman's son Jirang has been teaching me the basics, and when I say that I'd like to explore the klongs for a few hours, his eyes brighten and he says he'd like to come along to show me around. Andaman gives him some money and tells him to bring back some khao, or rice.

We walk to the end of the alleyway, and at the edge of the canal, we watch a procession of boats scurry back and forth. Jirang focuses on one, makes a special wave with his fingers, and it comes towards us. It is the klong equivalent of a public bus, complete with a sign that indicates the major stops it makes. We board, squeeze onto benches crammed with about fifty other people, and the driver revs the engine, re-entering the flow of river traffic at high speed. It is the same type of thin boat the papaya seller used, but longer, its bow draped with a lei of fresh flowers, an offering. It manoeuvres speedily through a labyrinth of canals, each looking as similar as the next, a maelstrom of waterways that would take a lifetime to learn well enough to navigate. I am in awe at the thought of a large part of the Bangkok population that grows up and spends its life on water instead of on pavement.

The city teems with life from its klongs. I see things that I might not otherwise see in a city—people washing their clothes at the back of their houses, preparing a meal in the kitchens that open out onto the klong, bathing children, girls talking and braiding each other's hair, a bare-chested boy fishing alone, deep in contemplation. The *klong* is the Thai equivalent of the Spanish courtyard. From the street side, the houses look plain, uninhabited, but when you pass through the gate to the courtyard behind the houses, you see a beauty hidden from the street, the life in daily routine, the things of consequence: food, conversation, moments of affection and emotion.

Jirang and I step off the boat at a wall crowded with people—we are at the base of a market, and I follow him through a throng of stalls hawking everything from barrettes to dried mushrooms. The sun has set, and the stalls are lit with strings of lamps. It seems as though all of Bangkok is here, mashed in between makeshift walls, buying bags of fresh fish for dinner, satchels for school, new blouses to wear to work, some toothpaste for themselves. There is no order. Jirang marches confidently through a mile or two of stalls piled high with fresh turmeric root, ginger's tangy cousin galangal, wonderful purple mangosteens that release a sticky sweet fragrance into the air. We wander past stalls selling only freshly made sauces, displayed in wide metal bowls. We pass young children making fried bananas, and ancient toothless women selling bunches of fresh herbs, sticky rice, and coconut custard baked in tiny pumpkins. We walk for hours, never tiring, and then suddenly Jirang stops in front of a stall and tells me that this is where we will buy the rice. The stall has baskets and baskets of it, two dozen varieties, raw or already steamed. In the same stall there is a sizzling wok into which a woman is throwing some tiny, pea-sized thai eggplants. She flips the mixture about and an aroma rises from it that has saliva springing into my mouth. She grabs a handful of basil, throws it in, and immediately tips the mixture into a steel container that a customer has brought for her to fill. I ask Jirang if he would like some and he nods. We tell her to make enough for two and she replaces the wok over the fire, adds oil and whole and ground pork, and starts all over again. In less than three minutes we have a meal.

Jirang and I make our way back to the water and sit at its edge, feet hanging over the side of the canal wall, watching boats and people blast past us. As we snack on our meal, Jirang tells me that Bangkok's canals used to outnumber its streets, but that many of them have been filled in and paved over.

In the middle of our discussion, a man approaches us and hands us a couple of bottles of Coke. We try to pay, but he won't let us. Jirang *wais* and shrugs at me. "*Mai pen lai*," he says—a favourite saying of the Thais and one of the first that he taught me; it means "what goes around comes around" or "don't worry" or "it's okay" or "doesn't matter." I hold the Coke in my hand and suddenly feel a heightened sensitivity about who I am (a westerner) and where I am (not in the West) and resent this collision of western culture with another, much more dynamic, one. It is a strange feeling, one that stays with me the whole way home, through the chaotic *klongs* and *sois* of this teeming Asian city.

∽

A woman feeds me a huge lunch among the corrugated iron shacks that line a canal. Her restaurant is the open kitchen/dining room/living room of her home, and I have the impression that anyone who wants something of hers for lunch, one of her specialties, just stops by and sits down, eats, and leaves. No exchange of words or cash or goods. It is all a mental tally and I imagine that the man sitting next to me has brought her the vegetables she is cooking with today, or that if she ever needed her stove fixed, all she would have to do is tell one of her regulars and he would fix it, no exchange of words or cash or goods.

She welcomes me with a grand smile and waves to the pots on her stove, asking me if I see anything I like. Three huge pots are steaming away next to the rice cooker. When I point to the curry chicken, she raises her eyebrow and lets out a burst of high-pitched air that sounds like an incredulous laugh, which she quickly suppresses. She sees that I am quite serious, and reaches for a small bowl, but she can't suppress her grin.

Throughout my meal, her eyes are fixed on me; she dishes out curry for her regulars without so much as giving them a nod. Surprisingly, it is not the incendiary curry that I had anticipated, but one lined with citrus, smoothly coconut-coated, with a nuance of spice. It slips down my throat in sensuous bursts of flavour and she is pleased. When I am finished, she does charge me, ten baht or fifty cents, a fraction of what I am willing to pay for a dish like that, because I can offer her no exchange, no promise of future service. I am a western tourist.

⁂

There is no simplicity in Thai food. It has a complex structure in which nothing can be replaced with something else. Substitute a lemon for lemongrass and it doesn't quite work. Throw in some lime zest instead of a lime leaf and it doesn't even resemble the dish you had in Bangkok. Thai food tastes the way it does because it uses ingredients that are not used in the same combination in any other cuisine or culture; its flavour is unique, strong, unyielding, like the Thais themselves. "Thais seem to thrive on the big bang of opposing tastes and textures coming at each other like express locomotives from different directions, only to meet headlong in one mighty, glorious explosion....The safe lines between savoury and sweet, so clear in the West, are just not taken seriously here," says Madhur Jaffrey in *A Taste of the Far East*.

That having been said, Thailand is a place where depending on where you are and whether you choose to support the collision of cultures, it is sometimes easier to find a hamburger or a doughnut or a western omelette than it is a nice steaming bowl of curry or a refreshing glass of grass jelly.

One cannot avoid being a tourist in Thailand. But the Thais gracefully welcome you into their world as easily as they provide you with an extension of your own, if you so desire.

It is late afternoon, and the satay vendors have all but disappeared from the streets, only to be replaced by fruit vendors. I pause to buy some rambutans and a piece of succulent skewered pineapple that is the very definition of the word "nectar." I still have a few hours to kill before boarding a night train to the south and decide to sit in a park and watch the goings-on. Soon the fruit vendors disappear and the noodle soup carts trundle in and set up. They are joined by more carts selling skewered deep-fried fish, pancakes with lychee paste, fish balls, drinks of condensed milk, ice and jelly, and then they are joined by more carts selling steamed rice with *nam pla*, fried shallots and an egg cracked on top, fish ball soup, skewered chicken parts. All around me people are eating and laughing. I think about how this sort of thing would occur in Canada only on a long weekend or in celebration of some anniversary: a birthday, a holiday, a wedding. I imagine how I would like to live in a place where laughing and eating food meant to electrify the senses are an almost hourly ritual. I close my eyes and grin at the thought.

On the way to the train station, I pass the affluent inching their way home in a rush hour that seems to merely be an extension of the rush hour I walked through this morning. Shiny chauffeured Jaguars stand and rumble beside sidewalk vendors who hawk anything and everything they have in their possession, all spread out on a sheet or blanket in front of them—a used toothbrush, a handful of bolts, credit cards, a pair of worn shoes, a few old coins. There is an unrecorded, unaccounted for commerce here —the life of Bangkok focuses strictly on providing the basics for its people. Nowhere has that been more evident to me than here. I walk along large, spotless boulevards housing tall, silvery glass skyscrapers that reflect a sun setting in a mustard-yellow smog; skyscrapers that hide the economy

Bangkok's bustle

which lies in the wranglers of food carts and boats in flotsam-laden *sois* and *klongs*. I wander along the wrong side of the wall of the golden tips and lustrous roofs of the Grand Palace, separated from throngs of pale, T-shirted and saronged tourists with video cameras recording flowers and monuments and saffron-robed monks. I pass corrugated metal shacks rusty from monsoons, plastic piled upon plastic: pink plastic bags stuffed with garbage on top of blue bags stuffed with food scraps on top of white bags stuffed with more plastic bags. The canal that once ran beside the shacks has long since been stopped with more garbage and broken baskets tossed from the dark open doorways on its banks, seething with filth and green, brackish water. In the grey and the slime and the eternal, choking detritus there is always a paradisaical palm grove or outcropping of banana plants seemingly thriving on or in the impurity, like the Thais themselves.

I walk slowly beneath highway overpasses, past more shacks, their insides filled with heavily greased auto parts being repaired for daily bread. Alongside a discarded truck axle sleeps a smooth-skinned boy wearing a pale green dimpled undershirt and no bottoms. The smell of incense lingers around the metal shacks and I see a miniature Buddha figure glowing bright red and shrouded with fresh flowers standing right next to a child who is spot-welding a muffler, sandwiched between two enormous piles of ball-bearings. As the child welds, his flame penetrating the darkness around him, the Buddha casts a comforting glow on the boy, more enveloping and diffusive than the harsh flame from the torch.

THAI RECIPES

Som Tam (Green Papaya Salad)

Green papayas are larger than sweet papayas and are not sweet at all.
They are usually available at Asian food markets, but if not,
substitute green mango or blanched green cabbage. Bird
chilis, fish sauce, palm sugar, and dried prawns will be available in Asian food markets too.

1 clove garlic
a large pinch of salt
3 bird chilis, fresh or dried
a handful of roasted peanuts
1 tbsp. fish sauce
juice of ½ lime
2 tsp. palm sugar
1 tbsp. dried prawns
2 plum tomatoes, chopped coarsely
1 lb. green papaya, peeled and sliced into
small julienned strips

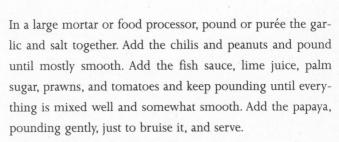

In a large mortar or food processor, pound or purée the garlic and salt together. Add the chilis and peanuts and pound
until mostly smooth. Add the fish sauce, lime juice, palm
sugar, prawns, and tomatoes and keep pounding until everything is mixed well and somewhat smooth. Add the papaya,
pounding gently, just to bruise it, and serve.

Serves 2 as a meal, 4 as a snack or appetizer.

Neua Pad Keemao (Stall-style Minced Beef Stir-fry)

This is a popular late-night snack on the streets of Bangkok. Bird chilis, lemongrass, palm sugar, and rice wine are available at any Asian food market. Cilantro with its roots still attached should be easy to find there too.

2 tbsp. oil
1 clove garlic, minced
½ inch fresh ginger, grated
2 bird chilis, fresh or dried, chopped
2 shallots, chopped
2 inches fresh lemongrass, chopped, or 2 tbsp. dried
   lemongrass
½ bunch cilantro, with roots, chopped
1 lb. minced beef
½ cup beef stock or water
2 tsp. palm sugar
2 tsp. soy sauce
2 tbsp. rice wine or sake
1 head lettuce, separated into leaves

Heat the oil in a large wok over high heat. Add the garlic, ginger, chilis, shallots and lemongrass and cook for 2 minutes. Add the cilantro and beef and cook for 3 to 4 minutes, breaking the beef up as you stir. Add the stock, palm sugar, soy sauce, and rice wine. Bring everything to a boil and cook for another minute. Serve in bowls with lettuce on the side for scooping.

Serves 4 as a snack.

Khao Tom

This is typically served for breakfast or as a late-night snack in Thailand. The condiments served with it vary from household to household, region to region. Lemongrass, jasmine rice, fish sauce, and dried shrimp are available at any Asian food market.

8 cups chicken stock or water
1 inch fresh ginger, grated
1 stalk fresh lemongrass, cut into 1-inch pieces,
    or 2 tbsp. dried lemongrass
3 shallots, chopped fine
1 cup jasmine rice
3 tbsp. fish sauce
nam pla prik (recipe follows)
dried shrimp
deep-fried shallots
roasted peanuts, chopped
a handful of cilantro or basil,
chopped coarsely

Bring the chicken stock, ginger, lemongrass, and shallots to a boil in a large pot over high heat. Stir in the rice, return to a boil, reduce the heat to medium-high and cook, stirring occasionally, for half an hour or so, until it has the consistency of porridge. Stir in the fish sauce and cook for a further 5 minutes. To serve, place the khao tom into large bowls and allow each person to sprinkle nam pla prik, dried shrimp, deep-fried shallots, peanuts, and chopped herbs over top.

Serves 4 for breakfast or as a light snack.

Nam Pla Prik

This condiment is ubiquitous in Thailand. It is used to give food zing
and is very easy to make. Fish sauce and bird chilis are available in Asian food markets.

1/2 cup fish sauce
a small handful of fresh or dried bird chilis, crushed

Mix together the fish sauce and chilis. Serve as a condiment.
Makes enough for 4.

GEORGIA

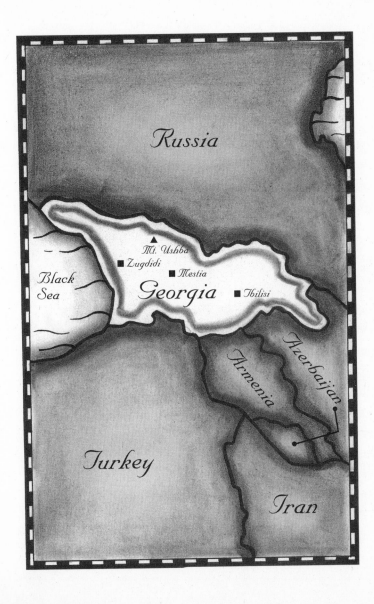

What a bizarre country! Each time I'm in a pretty landscape,
there's a church or a feast!
—Pascal Ichak, *A Chef in Love*

Every now and then, you stumble across a place so complex and unexpectedly wonderful that you know it will affect you for the rest of your life. Georgia is that place for me. It is everything: mountainous and flat, tropical and snow-covered, romantic and dangerous, chivalrous and chauvinistic, hospitable and desperate. But what prevails over every other characteristic is the spirit and vitality of its people.

You cannot be anywhere in Georgia without feeling its fierce pride. The word for "hello" in Georgian is "*Gamardzhoba,*" derived from its word for "victory." Such an evolution of language is significant in Georgia; it is a country that has endured more than forty incursions from all sides, religions, and notorious conquerors, as well as seventy years of communist rule and its fall, and a civil war shortly thereafter (with aftershocks still occurring) in which it gave up its northwestern province of Abkhazia and left ten per cent of Georgia's population as refugees. To have survived centuries of invasion with pride and culture still intact (if not even more entrenched) is something extraordinary, its people remarkable. It is a place that is difficult to be unaffected by, a piece of land sandwiched between the Black Sea and the Caspian, in a part of the world that is neither Europe nor Asia, but somewhere in between. Somewhere Georgian.

To add to this, the Georgians have a reputation for celebration and high-spiritedness, even in times of such upheaval. This was precisely why we were going. Georgia's reputation precedes itself.

Friends of ours who couldn't locate the country on a map all knew about the apparently endless festive drinking, singing, and feasting that Georgians are renowned for. This could only mean good news.

We were not prepared for the magnitude of celebration of life that met us. What we thought were surely exaggerated stories turned out to be grossly understated legends.

⁓

We enter Georgia from Turkey on a dismal day. We pass through customs, and as we wheel our bikes into a parking lot filled with Ladas, a large man, a civilian, emerges from one of the cars, shouting, "Welcome to Georgia!" He grabs me, kissing me squarely on the lips and shakes Doug's hand fervently. He gathers his friends around, and they run their hands over our bikes and gear, asking us where we are from. Slowly, each of them goes back to their cars and returns to us with something—a bag of apples, a bottle of vodka, some jam—pressing it in our hands and wishing us luck before letting us set off down the road.

Rain mists down over the Black Sea coast. We ride past building after abandoned building, all standing but stripped of anything of value: glass panes, wooden beams, baseboards, doors, electrical wiring. They are skeletons of concrete and rusted steel, slumped in the middle of verdant coastal plains surrounded by burgeoning fig and plum trees. We pass a huge Ferris wheel that has long since had its seats and decorations scavenged, and we find it ironic that the newly capitalist Georgians are forced to forage for goods that communism left behind. The deserted Ferris wheel spins eerily on rusty spindles in the breeze, creaking and moaning delicately, a leftover from an era not so long past, when this region was a playground for Soviet diplomats.

An hour or so up the coast we enter the town of Batumi, where women parade through the crowd at a busy market with large trays strapped to their bellies, shouting and pressing enormous wedges of cheese bread into the hands of their customers. Another woman stands inside a covered vehicle the size of an old milk truck. It is filled entirely with slender eggplants and she is knee-deep in them, grabbing plastic laundry baskets thrust at her from the throng in front of the truck. She fills them with ten, twenty, thirty pounds of eggplants while her assistant, brandishing a long-handled hoe, pulls forward more eggplants piled high out of reach in the back of the truck. She laughs at us when we ask for only two eggplants, then tosses them to us, shooing us away when we try to pay. Behind the truck there are tables spanning the length of a football field, mounded with an early autumn's harvest of carrots, peppers, onions, dill, cilantro, basil, potatoes, fresh yogurt and cheese, an abundance of food amid roofless, dilapidated buildings. If we buy anything that weighs under a pound, the vendors look at us bemusedly, then hand over the produce with a huge smile. When we try to pay, they will not accept anything.

On the road, hands flap at us out of windows of passing cars, and everywhere people shout in Russian "*Ot Kuda?!*" ("Where are you from?!"). Immediately, Georgian generosity is evident, almost heartbreaking. When we turn down a ride from a giant, he subsequently runs us off the road. He towers over us, shouting violently, swinging fake punches and trying to pull my bike helmet off my head. After our initial terror, we realize he is offended that we have refused his hospitality. He pours some vodka into our water bottles, claps Doug on the back, and drives on without us.

Half an hour later on the same road, we are flagged down by two men standing in front of a house. They forbid us to go any farther. They passed us near Zugdidi, they say, and waited an hour in their driveway for us to pass. Valari and Mehrab pull us into the house and begin to shout. Valari's wife emerges from the kitchen, takes one surprised look at us, and disappears. A few minutes later, she emerges again, her arms piled high with plates and bowls of *adzhapsandali* (a spectacular Georgian eggplant and potato stew reminiscent of ratatouille), cold bean salad, fresh fruit, flatbread, hazelnuts just picked from the bush outside and, of course, wine. She calls her two children and we sit down. After a lengthy, incomprehensible toast, we all tuck in and eat for hours, French style, a bit here, a bit there, wine and water to wash it all down. More people appear, and suddenly the house is full of even more food and vodka. Valari tries to make sense of who has arrived by introducing us to a variety of cousins, in-laws, and friends, and the local mechanic.

Mehrab, on the other hand, is a boisterous man who, with each new toast, challenges us to make him drink more than the last time. He wrinkles his nose in disgust when Doug speaks Russian to him. He tells us stories of his life in Georgian, of which we know not a single word. He delivers his stories with much arm-flailing, drawing diagrams in Doug's journal and reluctantly tossing in an occasional Russian word for our benefit, all with an air suggesting that we are innocent, we haven't seen anything compared to him (and indeed we haven't). He is a former mercenary-turned-cop who fought for the Soviet Union in Angola and Cuba, among other places, and reveals an intense hatred for all non-Georgians except, inexplicably, us. When the wine has lubricated him sufficiently, he takes off his shirt and points to seven scars, stretched purple rounds of healed skin, some surprisingly close to his heart, telling us the stories that came with each bullet he survived.

And so the evening goes. Six hours after we start, the feast is finished. Men stagger out of the house, singing, the children run about in their pyjamas in front of a television that blares the staticy noise of the only channel, a weak signal from Moscow. Mehrab gives us hug after breath-dissipating hug, bellowing that we will be lifelong friends. After he leaves, the house falls silent. Valari and his wife shake their heads and laugh, then drag themselves off to bed.

In the morning, we pedal away after a tearful and high-spirited goodbye and begin our ascent into the mountains. Decay takes on a new meaning. Gas and oil are sold in Mason jars from roadside stands. Soviet-era factories stand silent, everything of use stolen. The buildings are virtually see-through and the landscape that surrounds them is war-torn. Humanitarian aid trucks are omnipresent, weaving in and out of local traffic. A heavy mist continues to cling to everything as we pass a handful of military checkpoints manned by young Russian soldiers.

The traffic dissipates, the road worsens, and we spend the day climbing through clouds and rain in a spectacularly narrow valley. Doug calls it post-apocalyptic, so empty in all aspects that we have the feeling something catastrophic has happened and we should be on the lookout for survivors. The people we do see are walking on the road, seemingly from nowhere, ostensibly going somewhere that doesn't exist. We have not passed a settlement, or even a house, all day.

We climb and climb and slowly run out of energy. Towards dusk, we pass a small village of about fifty houses. As we are filling our water bottles at a stream, we see a man standing in a field and we shout over to him, asking him if he knows of a place where we can camp for the night. "Of course!" he shouts back. He wades through the field towards us and leads us along a narrow, precipitous path to his house. He gives us his room to sleep in. It is filled with reams of old newspapers, black and white photos, and a portrait of Stalin (still revered in Georgia) smoking a pipe. He cuts some home-made bread and pours some wine and makes us a salad of fresh-picked tomatoes, chervil, dill, parsley, and salt. Before we know it, the neighbours have joined us. This is a special occasion, they say, as they cook up a stew with a piece of freshly slaughtered bear. For dessert they produce a slab of precious chocolate.

As we eat, Wassaw tells us that for seventeen years, he was the principal of the school in this small town and one of the neighbours was a teacher of Russian literature. The school had about thirty-five students, he says, but the government shut it down five months ago because there was no money to pay anyone. He and his neighbour shrug. There is nothing they can do. They shrug again and laugh when Doug asks how they survive. "I am still here," says Wassaw, "look around you." He sweeps his hand across the room. "Everyone is in the same boat. Life is simple in the mountains. It's much easier here than in the city."

Wassaw asks if we know the Georgian creation legend. Doug and I shake our heads. "No? Well," he says, dusting his hands, "I'll tell you and then perhaps you will understand."

"When God was distributing land, the Georgians were overlooked because they were busy drinking, feasting and generally being, well, Georgian," Wassaw says, hoisting his glass of wine. "When they found out that they had not been given any land, the Georgians approached God and begged Him to reconsider. He asked them why they had not been present when He was dividing everything up, and the Georgians replied, 'Why, we were celebrating life and your existence!' God considered this and said to them, 'There is one piece of land left, and since I know what kind of people you are and since you were occupied in such a noble endeavour, I'll give it to you.' It was the piece of land, you realize, that God had saved for himself, the most beautiful corner of the world, with magnificent mountains, with wonderful plains, and with good soil for growing all the fruits and vegetables we could ever need and most importantly, the grapes with which we make our famous wine." He holds his glass up again and we toast the wisdom of God, realizing just "what kind of people" Georgians are.

In this small village, which could easily be mistaken for one in Switzerland, with peaks rising high into the clouds and houses built on small patches of flat land, people grow their own tomatoes, milk their cows, raise some hens, kill a bear every now and then, and have what they have and nothing more. They make their own cheese, bread, vodka, and wine and they accept their predicament. Times are always hard for the Georgians, so life gets pared down, becomes simple. The most important thing is to have wine with one's food every day, and the Georgians are resourceful enough to be self-sufficient in that respect. This is what allows their dignity and spirit to remain not only intact but vibrant.

The next morning we continue our knee-aching climb on the narrow road, which can only be described as a quagmire of mud. Few cars tackle this road from Dvaria to Mestia, and those that do take it at a pace not much faster than our bikes. We follow the curves of the mountain, whose sides are so steep that one slip of the pedal will send either one of us tumbling head over wheels into the Inguri River a few thousand feet below. Alps-type villages dot the narrow valley floor far beneath us. Snow-capped peaks and glaciers appear as clouds lift, and the sun warms us while we climb higher into the mountains.

We ride towards the town of Mestia and spot the first of the region of Svaneti's renowned stone towers. They are over a thousand years old, built by families who would retreat to them during the violent feudal times that Svans are famous for. The towers are impenetrable, poking up here and there from precipices and stone outcroppings, built high to track intruders. In towns they now stand among modern buildings, most of them still perfectly intact, a testament to their strength.

We arrive in the centre of Mestia, a square saddened by post-Soviet times, abandoned save for six identical sagging kiosks sitting in a row, all selling the same selection of soap, sprats, cookies, and Turkish chocolate bars. Signs hang listlessly from one screw. In a small park, the legs of a bench are tilted so much from years of use and disrepair that, although the seat remains parallel to the ground, it sits only a few inches above it. Leaves from several autumns clutter the grass. A handful of uniformed men stand smoking and chatting outside of what must be the police station. Each of their uniforms looks completely different from the others; one is a grey camouflage, well-worn but neatly pressed; another is light green, thin and threadbare; yet another is navy blue... a patchwork of military clothing gathered from various sources for Georgia's finest.

One of the soldiers approaches us and asks where we are from. We tell him, but he is disappointed that we are only Canadian. He wants something more political, defining, like the Americans who gave him the "Don't Mess with Texas" pin he wears on his lapel. We have somehow touched him, though, and he suggests a tour of the police arsenal. It's an opportunity that doesn't come up very often, so we agree. He leads us inside the building, into a bunkroom, where he opens lockers and drags trunks out from under beds. Here, tucked between the T-shirts and blankets and love letters and pictures from home are Kalashnikovs and missile launchers and bazookas and grenades. I'm not much of a gun person, but the soldier puts a weighty flak jacket and helmet on me nonetheless and asks if I'd like to hold his machine gun. I am reluctant for one moment too long so he throws it to me, drags me to the window, and tells me to look through the scope. "One kilometre," he says, telling me its range and pointing to the hill in the distance. He grabs the gun and, with a series of quick hand movements and loud crunches of metal, loads it. He looks through the scope for a while, focuses on something, then tells me to look through the scope again. One kilometre away, on the hillside, an old man walks slowly along a path, completely unaware that a loaded gun is pointed at him. The soldier pushes me, tells me to fire if I want to. Shaking, I hand the gun back to him. He laughs and, frustrated with my cowardice, offers to take Doug down to the river to fire a shot from his Kalashnikov, where no one will be hurt. Half an hour later

Doug returns, clutching a still-warm shell. He, having never fired a gun in his life, got a bull's-eye.

We ask the soldier where the rest of his colleagues are. He shrugs and says that they are with the commander, picking wild mushrooms somewhere in the forest. He has been left behind to make sure that everything runs smoothly, which now seems to include showing us to the 'museum' in town. It is the house of Georgian mountaineering wonder Mikhail Kirgiani, and has been turned into an archive of his accomplishments. The interior of the family's stone tower has been converted into a re-enactment of his fatal fall in the 1960s, snapped rope and all. The director and guide of the museum, Sasha, is a mountaineer himself and a highly respected citizen of Mestia who speaks a mélange of English, German, and French, all at once. "Eeehm… Kirgiani… eeehm… klettert on der montagne in Russia," he says, pointing to a photo of an expedition in the 1950s. "Frau of Kirgiani, and brother und pere… " pointing to a picture of his family. After leading us through all the displays of expeditions, he offers us a room to stay in just off the museum, and smiles and shakes his head slowly when we ask what we can pay him.

That evening, a parade of people stand, sit, and walk through our room, barely acknowledging us, preferring to go straight to Sasha to ask who we are, where we are from, how long we are staying. They bring us bowls and plates of food sent over from their homes. The whole town is steeped in preparing the funeral feast of a young man who has just died, and dishes of beet salad, a cold potato, onion and coriander mash, bean stew, fresh flatbread, and a sweet millet porridge are piled on us. I ask a girl about the man who has died and I am told that he was only sixty. She asks what life expectancy is in Canada, and I feel ashamed to say eighty. Everyone in the room shakes their heads and says, "So young, so young. In Georgia, we live until we are one hundred and twenty." And then I remember that I have heard this before, that this region is reputed to have the highest percentage of centenarians in the world.

One of the men brings some arak, an alcoholic drink made from stale bread, water, and yeast. It has a slightly sour, diluted grain alcohol taste, but is not as strong as schnapps or vodka. I am allowed a taste, but Doug is required to take at least ten shots with the man who brought it, the logic being, I suspect, that if you've had ten shots, you may as well keep on going. Doug somehow manages to beg off after seven.

The parade through our room continues and in the midst of all the young men, a woman named Yamsi is brought to the door. She is studying languages at the university in Tbilisi and asks us in English all the questions we have spent the evening ineffectively answering with our smattering of Russian. She does not translate back to the others in the room, but they seem satisfied that we are at least communicating with her without a dictionary, answering and asking without hesitation. At the end of the evening, Yamsi insists that we go for a hike in the mountains the next day. "Otherwise," she says, "you will not understand Mestia the way you should."

Even after Sasha begs everyone to leave, knocks on our door continue past midnight. When I answer them, young men crowded onto the stone step outside stare blankly at me without saying anything, as if they had expected someone else.

～

Yamsi arrives in the morning with her brother and Sasha's sister, Maia. We begin our walk up steep slopes, towards an old Orthodox church with an earthen floor and no windows. It is still in use and so dark inside that a candle must be lit to see the shrine and altar. It is a powerful place without natural light... a narrow, oblong room that would accommodate about a dozen people, single file, all facing the shrine. We are crouched over and forced into whispers because of the claustrophobic feeling of the place. There are bones and skeletons beneath us, says Yamsi, in an open catacomb—the predecessor to the overgrown cemetery outside that is replete with headstones weathered and tipped by avalanches that roar through the town each winter.

We climb past sour plum trees and abundant hazelnut bushes into alpine pastures, chewing on fresh, milky nuts for sustenance, walking up and over rolling yellow hills to a cabin perched on a slope-side with a view of four or five different mountain faces freshly doused in snow.

The cabin is the summer home of two families from Mestia, a one-room log structure with dirt floors, a wood-burning stove, and a long monk's table for eating. Five rickety old beds placed side by side, each laden with a mass of wool blankets, take up most of the cabin's room. The families are distant cousins of Yamsi, and they live simply but well. They bring their cows and pigs and chickens up to the alpine pastures in the spring, when the snow has cleared, and plant potatoes, herbs, onions, cabbages and beets. They harvest eggs from their chickens and make their own cheeses and yogurt with milk from their cows. They use the fruit from the huckleberry, blueberry, and raspberry bushes tucked behind the hazelnut and plum outcroppings that we saw farther down the mountain. The only thing they need that they cannot grow themselves is wheat for flour, but a couple of fifty-pound sacks brought up in the spring will usually last them until the snow comes and the cows stop producing milk, which is when they bring everything back down to Mestia again.

Tina and Nana, the two young women in the family, emerge from the cabin when they hear our voices. They greet us with immense joy and invite us in, immediately settling down to make a special lunch. We spend a couple of hours asking each other questions, exhausting poor Yamsi, who is translating between Russian, Georgian, and English while the women chatter and laugh and knead dough. The three men of the family arrive, galloping in on horses, shotguns slung over their shoulders, like something out of a Western. The clouds rise and fall in the valley, allowing us a brief glimpse of Mount Ushba, a stone's throw away across the Russian border. The wind is cool, the air is fresh, and the sun makes us feel deliciously warm and lazy. We sit down to a high-dairy lunch, squeezing in at the monk's table, feasting on fresh ricotta-like cheese, older cheese aged in whey like feta, a mashed potato and cheese stew and *khachapuri*, the ubiquitous Georgian cheese bread. For dessert there is the most wonderful of Georgian things: *matsoni*. It is a thickened yogurt, usually made of buffalo's milk, and I am encouraged to mix it with a little fresh jam and drink. It tastes like fresh, rich cream spread over the most fragrant strawberry fields on earth.

The women shout cheerfully after us when we leave, and the men follow for a while on their horses, showing us a different way home, switchbacking down the backside of the mountain to the river. We walk and walk and walk, hoping that the clouds over Ushba will lift again.

"I love Mestia," Yamsi says, gazing at the view while we take a break. "My family is here. It's where I grew up. But I don't think I will live here again." Doug and I look over at her. She points across the river to Mestia's overgrown airstrip and a large hotel that at one time must have been marvellous, but now appears to be a bombed-out shell. The prospects are limited in rural Georgia, she says, even in a town of five thousand people. Mestia was once highly touristed, renowned for its mountain grandeur and beauty, but there are fewer than fifty tourists a year now, and the town has not seen mail or telephone service for more than four years, since the civil war in Abkhazia. "I have an aunt and grandmother who were living there," she says calmly, "but there is no way to know if they are still alive, or if they are now refugees in some other part of Georgia." Suddenly I understand that perhaps the Georgian resilience exists as a way of masking pain.

We reach Mestia at nightfall, pausing for a sip of water from the town's spring, and follow a group of woodsmen bearing heavy-handled axes on their shoulders back into town. Yamsi invites us to her house for a brief introduction to her family, and they greet us graciously. The ages of her eight brothers and sisters span thirty years. She feeds us some roasted potatoes with tkemali, a wonderful sauce made from sour plums and chilis that tastes like tart, cooked apples with a spicy kick. Just as we are about to leave, Yamsi's father arrives, more than a little drunk because he and some others have spent the day building the dead man's coffin and mourning him. He is very emotional and begins to weep with happiness when he sees Yamsi, then claps his hands loudly and dramatically, signalling that it is time for a drink, since there are guests in his house. The family giggles at him and tries to put him to bed. We thank Yamsi for a spectacular day and walk back to our room in the museum, feeling as though we know a little bit more of Georgia.

⌒

We decide to leave the mountains and head for the hills that Georgia shares with Azerbaijan. It is from here that Georgia's famous wine comes, where grapes have been growing and wine has been made for thousands and thousands of years. Some Georgians insist that cuttings from some of the vines here were transported to Europe a few centuries ago, where they now produce France's grand vins.

We stop in a small town just where the vineyards begin. Doug is immediately reined in by some merchants and given a glass of cloudy, greyish wine, a mug of beer, and an enormous shopping bag full of eggplants, peppers, and onions, as well as two watermelons. Refusing it is not an option. As we try to rearrange our baggage to strap the watermelons onto our already listing load, everyone wants to give us more. We wobble down the road to the next village, which we have heard is famous for producing some of Georgia's best wine. There is not much sign of life in the vineyards, so we pull off the road and ask some women where we can buy some wine. One of them goes off to fetch a bottle from her house. She, of course, will not let us pay for it, so we give her one of the water-melons and ride on down the valley to the next town.

The road is lined with walnut trees, and all morning we watch and listen as people pull up to them in their cars, detach long sticks from the roof, climb into the trees, and whack the branches to loosen the walnuts from their stems. The shoulder of the road is packed with cars and with children running under the trees collecting the fallen nuts. The hollow smack of sticks on walnut resonates through the air. Farther down the road, a wine harvest has begun and the vineyards are busy with chatter and people filling buckets full of grapes.

We start to coast down through a lush, green canyon. A crammed minivan passes us, and one of the passengers gives us the thumbs-up sign out the window, a rare and surprising signal in Georgia. Around a corner, the minivan has stopped, its passengers standing on the side of the road, waving for us to pull over. One of the passengers is Canadian, a lawyer named Chris who is teaching at the university in Tbilisi. He tells us that the dean of the university wants to invite us to a traditional wine harvest and feast in a town farther down the valley—they are already late, but give us directions and drive off in a flurry.

An hour later, after riding through undulating hills and vineyards, we arrive in the main square of Vanta. It is deserted, except for two teenagers sitting in a car. They honk at us and tell us that they live in the house we are supposed to go to and have been placed there to collect us. The minivan crew is in the vineyard picking grapes, but we are taken to the house and made welcome. As we are shown into the courtyard, a man emerges from the vineyard carrying two decanters of white wine and about a dozen loaves of boat-shaped bread. He greets the teenagers with crushing hugs and immediately orders the boys to get some glasses. He pours wine into them, muttering a brief toast. We raise our glasses and drink while he tells us that he is the mayor of this "town" (he merely sweeps his hand across the horizon when describing his constituency) and that he came to welcome us and celebrate.

The others arrive shortly, introductions are made again, and the production of wine begins. A farm tractor backs a large trailer full of grapes into the door of the house and everyone begins scooping them into pails and buckets. The grapes are carried into a dark room with a dirt floor, beneath which a three thousand-litre clay amphora was sunk over a hundred years ago. A hand-cranked mill sits over top of the mouth of the amphora and pail by pail the grapes, stems and all, are pulverized and released into the mammoth buried jug. The more grapes are crushed, the more people begin to arrive, each taking an obligatory turn at the mill, cranking for their right to celebrate the harvest and feast.

Finally there are no more grapes to crush, and we are carried along into a room that has an enormous banquet table. It is crammed with so many dishes that a few threaten to teeter over the edge: dishes of smoked fish, walnut paste, salted fresh green beans, more bread and cheese, a spectacular string bean and tomato stew, roasted eggplant slices with garlic and parsley sprinkled over top, roasted potatoes with tkemali, and the ubiquitous tomato, cucumber, hot pepper, parsley, and salt salad. We are, of course, expected to polish off the remainder of last year's wine (which seems a vast amount)—hence the reason for the feast: to make way for the new stuff. There are about sixty people at the table and we are all shushed as the tamada, the toastmaster, makes his first toast, to a fine harvest.

The tamada is usually the host of the party, the man of the house, and it is his job to perform the most important toasts—to thank the appropriate deities for a plentiful harvest and a proliferation of food and wine. He does so with great, lengthy philosophical speeches, throughout which, as a guest, you are allowed to eat but not drink.

Once the *tamada* has finished his toast, he looks around the room and everyone tips their enormous glasses down their throats.

Somehow the table seems twice as full of food as it did when we sat down. The toasts become longer and longer, infused with lyrical Georgian folk songs played wonderfully and energetically on the national instrument, a small bulbous guitar with four strings. Everyone sings boldly, as though they practise every day, songs of love, love for family, a specific person, their country, unity. At the end of a folk song celebrating war, one of the women at the table allows herself to cry a bit for a brother who died in Abkhazia in the civil war.

In between all the singing, the *tamada* toasts his house and family and, separately, the women who spent three days cooking all of this wonderful food. We eat. We toast. We drink. We listen and nibble and sip until our heads loll atop our bloated bodies. Just when we think it is over, a woman emerges with a pedestal of fresh figs, pomegranates, pears, melons, and wonderful walnuts, which the mayor proceeds to crack open with bare hands, despite our whimpering protests. The

The post-feast feast at the wine harvest celebration

table looks like a painting of cornucopia and debauchery, simultaneously plentiful and demolished with pleasure.

By 5:30, three hours after we sat down to eat, the *tamada* breaks down and allows others to make toasts. The toasts become ridiculous: to the sky, to the trees, to children not yet born. Chris and Doug realize they have met before, in northern Ontario, a long time ago. And so it goes. At 7 p.m., the minivan crew staggers away back to Tbilisi (with a sober driver), and Doug and I beg off any more food or drink and crawl into bed, bellies like watermelons. The elders carry on, and we are woken occasionally by roars of more toasts and drunken song sung well past midnight.

By 7 a.m., the teenagers have been roused and are playing basketball outside by the grape arbour. After a few of the hungover guests complain, Grandma tells them to go away for a while. They take us up to their old school to continue the game, which turns into soccer because the school does not have a basketball net. After an hour or so, we head back to the house.

We arrive to find that a large table in the arbour has been set with what seems like more food and wine than yesterday. It is 8:30 in the morning, the guests have risen and, though groggy, they hang onto the *tamada*'s every word as he begins his first toast of the day. We start with wine, move on to vodka, and two of the women stagger out of the kitchen under the weight of an enormous pot of tripe soup, a well-known cure for hangovers. There is more eggplant, more beans, more potatoes, more bread, more cheese. The toasting continues: to Canadian-Georgian relations, to the future of students, to cows for providing fertilizer...

The man sitting beside me sighs and shakes his head. I ask him what the matter is. He throws his hands up in the air. "Things have changed."

"Things always change," Doug says, and everyone agrees.

"No, no... Georgians have changed. We aren't like we used to be.

Sure, times are always tough, but this time... this time we have really been affected."

"What do you mean?" I ask.

"Ten years ago, we were friendly, and hospitable. But now," he shakes his head in dismay. "I don't know. Everything is harder. We are harder. We don't have the desire for life that we used to." Doug and I stare at him in disbelief. Everyone else at the table nods in contemplation. "Oh well," says the *tamada*, hoisting his glass. "To desire for life." Everyone cheers and laughs loudly, drinks their wine and refills their glasses, telling Doug and me that we will have to stay for another day.

The party finally dissipates in the afternoon. We wind our way slowly back to Tbilisi and poke each other's swollen bellies, holding our swirling heads in our hands and laughing in the spirit of the Georgians, who have taught us so well to be thankful and grateful, to love life and take the bad with a grain of salt. And though we both know that because of this country and its extraordinary people we will never live our lives the same way we did before, we also know that somehow we will only be able to relay a fragment of our emotion for this place to the next unsuspecting traveller. Some things are best left unsaid.

GEORGIAN RECIPES

Tkemali

Tkemali is a wonderfully pungent sour plum sauce, served in Georgia over roasted chicken, fish, pork, and potatoes. It is traditionally made with plums that grow only in Georgia, but a close alternative are Santa Rosa plums, or any type of sour plum you can find. It keeps indefinitely in the refrigerator.

2 lb. plums (underripe Santa Rosas or Kelseys), cut in quarters
    and pits removed
1/2 cup vinegar
1/2 cup water
juice of 1 lemon
2 cloves garlic
1 tsp. coriander seed
1 tsp. fennel seed
1 red chili pepper (or 1 tsp. dried red chili flakes)
3/4 tsp. salt
2 tbsp. fresh mint
1/2 cup fresh cilantro

Place the plums in a saucepan with the vinegar, water, and lemon juice. Bring to a boil and simmer for 15 to 20 minutes, until softened, stirring occasionally to prevent it from burning. Place the garlic, coriander, fennel, chili, salt, mint, and cilantro in a food processor and blend into a paste. Add the plums and their liquid to the food processor and blend until smooth. Use immediately, or pour into jars and store in the refrigerator. Terrific over roasted potatoes!
Makes about 3 cups.

Khachapuri

This fabulous cheese bread is sold all over Georgia, in varying forms—the types of cheeses used for the filling can be mild or pungent, as long as they melt well, and the dough can be anything from a pizza-like bread to a fine puff pastry. This recipe creates something in between—a flaky, yet dense pastry, enjoyed on its own, or alongside a great stew or salad.

2 1/4 cups flour
1/2 tsp. salt
3/4 cup butter, chilled and cut into small pieces
2 eggs
1/2 cup plain yogurt
1/2 lb. Havarti cheese, grated
1/2 lb. feta cheese, crumbled
2 tbsp. fresh mint, cilantro, or parsley, chopped
1 egg, beaten with 1 tbsp. water

Heat the oven to 350°F. Combine the flour, salt, and butter in a large bowl and rub the mixture between your hands until crumbly (this is also easily done in a food processor or mixer). Add one egg and the yogurt and mix until a ball is formed. Roll out the dough into a rectangle of 1/4 inch thickness. Mix together the second egg, cheeses, and mint and spread over half the dough. Fold the dough over the cheese mixture to cover it and seal the edges by crimping them with a fork or your fingers. Beat the remaining egg and water together and brush the dough with it. Bake on a greased baking sheet for about an hour, until the dough is golden brown. Let the bread cool slightly. Cut into wedges or squares and serve while still warm.

Makes one square, to serve 6 to 8 as a snack or part of a meal.

Adzhapsandali

This is Georgia's version of ratatouille, with a twist. If you have a garden, you'll realize this dish exists because everything in it ripens at the same time. The potatoes give it texture and depth, the cayenne and paprika give the dish good heat, and the fresh herbs stirred in at the end really set it apart. It is simple to make and, like all good things, even better the next day.

1/4 cup oil
1 large eggplant, chopped
2 potatoes, peeled and cubed
3 tomatoes, chopped
1/2 cup water or red wine
4 cloves garlic, peeled and chopped
1 green pepper, cored and chopped
1 onion, peeled and chopped
salt and pepper to taste
1/2 cup minced fresh herbs (equal parts basil, dill, parsley,
    and cilantro)
pinch cayenne pepper
1/4 tsp. paprika

Heat the oil in a large pot or high-sided saucepan over medium-high heat. Add the eggplant and cook for 5 minutes. Add the potatoes, tomatoes, and water and cook for 10 to 15 minutes, until the potatoes are tender and the tomatoes and eggplant are beginning to fall apart. Add the garlic, green pepper, and onion and reduce heat to medium-low. Cover and let simmer for 10 minutes. Season, add the remaining ingredients, and let it all cook uncovered for 10 minutes or so, until most of the liquid has thickened. Georgians eat this at room temperature, but it's quite all right to serve it hot if you can't wait for it to cool.

Serves 4 for lunch or a light dinner.

TURKEY &
ARMENIA

Turkey is melodramatic, in its colours, politics, religion, secularism. All its flavours stick with me and resurface daily, even when I am five thousand miles from it. It is the only place I have ever felt bathed simultaneously in aroma, sound, colour, and the history of several empires. The wailing of muëzzins reverberates through air saturated with the smell of tea and spices, calls to prayer bounce from minaret to minaret so hauntingly that I remember them now with absolute clarity.

We walk through Istanbul, mesmerized by a sensuousness that the constant breeze carries over the Golden Horn: the smell of coffee and apple blossoms, the sound of religious devotion emanating from the tops of minarets, the view of water everywhere, the taste of Asia, and the feel of Europe, all in the same place. I stand in mosques, staring up at the nipples of domes from their intricately tiled interiors, in edifices that carry a historical importance difficult to comprehend as it should be comprehended, but that easily overwhelm. The Turks seem bored by the role their Byzantium, their Constantinople, their Istanbul has played in shaping the world, perhaps because here the relics of those eras are so pervasive. One enters the archaeological museum after passing through a grassy graveyard of tumbled capitals, columns, and sarcophagi—the rejects of an already crammed public space. In the Basillica Cistern there are 336 of these "leftover" columns and capitals, among them two ancient heads of Medusa half-sunk in water, stone snakes trolling about the algaed, alabaster faces, a reminder of the empires that have affected this place.

The impossibly engineered divine church of Aya Sofya is being restored, but even with scaffolding distorting its intended effect, I stand beneath the peak of its enormous, seemingly suspended dome and cannot help but gape. It represents Turkey in all its phases: built in the sixth century as the greatest church in all Christendom; converted to a mosque during the Ottoman empire; no longer used as a place of religion today, but open to tourists whose admission fees will help pay for a restoration likely to last more than half a century.

The grand homes and mini-palaces that line the Bosphorus are all boarded up, curtains drawn, abandoned for centuries, it seems. Even in this rare glimpse of shabbiness, the grandeur of Istanbul pushes through and I wonder what it must have been like to approach the city from the sea, to sail into a rising, misty silhouette of minarets, churches, and the domes of mosques, to smell unknown spices and to hear for the first time the muëzzins' call to prayer float across azure water, the landscape a hazy orange.

And then there is the food. Wherever we turn in Istanbul there is a glimpse of it. Bridges are lined with men tending fishing poles where the Golden Horn meets the Bosphorus. Doug buys small thin fish straight off the hook, and a man in an old fishing trawler offers to cook them for us. I wait as his boat belches out greasy fumes at us, then almost faint at the taste of creatures so fresh they have only just closed their eyes in sacrifice. Booths line the concrete waterway behind us, selling vişne, the freshest, tartest sour cherry juice you can imagine. Old men push weathered painted carts, offering rings of sesame bread called simit and tiny cheese pastries called börek. Our mouths water as a man at one of the larger booths makes us lahmacun. He spreads oil, spices and meat paste over a thin piece of flatbread, rolls it up into a loose cone, and stuffs its centre with handfuls of fresh cilantro and parsley. The flavour is Turkey: multidimensional, coy and luring, steamy, seductive, like nothing I have ever tasted and certainly like nothing I had ever expected.

～

We board a small ship and sail past abandoned fortresses to the northern mouth of the Bosphorus, swing east and chug along the southern shore of the Black Sea, occasionally spotting minarets poking up from hillsides. The crew moves slowly and lamentfully along the decks; this is the ship's last voyage, put to death by Turkey's ever-expanding and efficient bus system. A sense of camaraderie gradually develops though, and by the time we disembark at Samsun thirty-six hours later, the funereal atmosphere has taken on tones of Mardi Gras, a celebration of the ship's purposeful lifetime. We stand on the concrete wharf between containers waiting to be loaded onto freighters and wave and wave and wave as the ship slips out of Samsun harbour for the last time. We mount our bikes and begin to ride away from the coast.

We climb through lush green hills that turn grassy, then straw-coloured, then dusty, then brown. We wipe tears from our cheeks as we ride through fields of harvested onions. We sleep peacefully behind a stone wall that marks an olive grove in the middle of a piece of deserted land. When the farmer discovers us in the morning, we apologize for camping in his field. He looks at us strangely, laughs, stretches his arms out and walks slowly in a circle. "It's only land," he says, offering his hand. "Welcome to Turkey."

We ride down through pink, rubbly mountains into a town where old men drinking tea from tulip-shaped glasses beckon us off the road and into the tea house. They bring us boiled eggs and fresh bread, point at the sun, and shake their heads at our bikes. The one o'clock call to prayer rings out and bounces around the walls of mountains that contain the town, resonating faintly for what seems like half an hour. A man brings everyone more tea. He points to the remnants of fortresses scattered along the ridges and brings his finger down mid-mountain to a series of enormous tombs carved into a sheer slope, a thousand feet or so above the town. I look around at this roadside tea house and see an almond tree, a plum tree, a quince tree, an apple tree, and a pomegranate tree, all heavily laden with fruit.

We decide to stay and wander beneath the vertical mountains all day, absorbed in the eeriness of each echoing call to prayer. I wake at 4:30 the next morning because of it, peer out of our tent, and see the tombs grandly lit; eyes of light in a town awash in darkness. I fall in love.

In the morning, we follow a wide river valley that bumps down to a small town where more men drinking tea flap their hands quickly at us and call us to join them. *"Chaichaichaichaichaichaichai!"* they shout as we pass. We rest and have lunch in the shade of poplars. A large truck drives by, shrieks to a halt, makes a U-turn that nearly tips itself onto two wheels, and pulls up beside us. The driver hops out, greets us in Turkish, and proudly holds up a large striped Santa Claus melon. Without warning, he slams it to the ground and it cracks. He rips it open with his hands and a lovely, thick, fragrant juice spills out. I toss him my knife and he babbles incessantly, asking us questions in Turkish (and answering them himself) while he cuts the melon into wedges. He wipes my knife on his pant leg. He takes a small piece of melon for himself, shouts a farewell, hops back into his truck, makes another precarious U-turn, and drives off, leaving us sticky-fingered and speechless. The melon bathes us in a perfume of honeyed nectar.

We continue riding, changing river valleys, and start to climb in a searing, unrelenting heat. We abandon our bikes and scurry down to the river's edge, dunking our bodies and then drying off on warm rocks. We eat freshly picked and roasted pistachios as children shoot past us in the water, heads bobbing and disappearing in frothy rapids. They giggle, and shriek, shouting for us to join them as the water carts them quickly downstream.

For the rest of the afternoon, we cycle and dunk, cycle and dunk. We take our cue from the Turks, who leap from their fields or their trucks or their cars into rapidly moving rivers when the heat becomes unbearable. They sigh in refreshment, shake the water from their heads and, dripping wet, get on with hoeing the field or driving to Ankara or herding sheep or picking fruit.

⌒

We're standing on the side of the road, exhausted, looking at our map. We have been riding all day, with no rivers to dunk ourselves into, the heat more oppressive than ever. A few hundred metres off the highway, on a small road into a town where we thought we might stay there is a barricade of sandbags, oil drums, and soldiers-in-training sporting AK-47s. A checkpoint. Not the best place to spend the night. It seems an odd thing, but there are times when you waltz into mud so thick that by the time you notice, it has anchored you and it is too late to get out.

We decide to ride farther down the highway and soon spot a grove of trees good for camping. On the other side of the road there is a tiny, sleepy railway station and Doug wanders inside to ask if we can fill our water bottles there. A little girl watches me as I wash my hands under the outdoor tap that her father has shown us. She wrinkles her nose at us, looks at our salt-encrusted faces, and asks if we want to have a bath. No, no, Doug says. We just need some water for cooking. He makes the motion of stirring a pot.

Her eyes widen at the sight of our loaded bicycles and she runs into the station, bringing a string of people out with her: brothers, sisters, aunts, the stationmaster. They look at the bikes, then at us as we fill our water bottles at the tap. The little girl says something to them, points to the bikes, then at the sky, and everyone nods. The stationmaster, a rosy-cheeked and impeccably dressed young man, asks us in perfect English where we will stay.

"We have a tent," says Doug. "We'll just camp somewhere."

The stationmaster translates to the rest of the group. Hands are thrown up in protest and words are muttered in disapproving tones. They huddle, discussing, and then move over to the bikes and wheel them inside the station. Doug and I exchange questioning looks. The stationmaster comes over and motions us forward.

"Come, come," he says. "We have plenty of room. If you really want to camp, you can camp out back."

A slew of chairs are brought out onto the platform and we all sit, looking up and down the tracks and listening to the birds chirp. Introductions are made: there is Mesmut, the stationmaster, who is just eighteen and who has been brought to this train station from Istanbul to straighten things out. There are his colleagues, Osman and Kemal, both about forty, who are extremely nice, but whom Mesmut confides are a little inefficient and not so energetic. There are their wives, who speak only Kurdish and, of course, the children: two teenage girls, one boy of about ten, the little girl, and a tiny baby who giggles without rest. Then there is the lonely old woman walking up and down the tracks, wailing Kurdish folk songs and glaring at all of us with horrified eyes.

"She is crazy," says Mesmut. "She is old and crazy. She does this all day, up and down. She lives down there, by the turn in the tracks. She has nothing to eat so we take care of her." Mesmut tells her that there is food inside and that she should go and eat something, but she waves him away impatiently. He shrugs. She turns and wanders down the tracks, singing softly to no one, wiping ancient tears from her cheeks.

After a while, we are called out to the back, where the men light a fire and begin roasting peppers and whole eggplants. We skin them as we talk about Turkey. Osman and Kemal want to know what we think of Turkey and if everyone has treated us well. They tell us that they are "neutral Kurds" (Kurds living in a non-Kurdish part of Turkey who do not favour either side of the on-going conflict). Mesmut glances behind us, where camouflaged soldiers in a military jeep move slowly into the hills. Its lethargy and stealth and the glow of the rear lights send a chill through me, not of unease, but of a failure to understand. Mesmut shakes his head and confides what most Turks and Kurds have confided to us: that the Turkish army justifies its movements by making the PKK (Kurdistan Workers Party) out to be more monstrous than it really is. He points up to the mountain tops. "They will go up there and spend the night looking for PKK, even though this is not Kurdish territory. They will fire a few shots at nothing and come down in the morning and go up again the next night." He sighs in resignation.

The men thread meat onto skewers and place them over the fire to roast, expertly flicking and turning them, like a rotisserie. I am shepherded into the living room, where the women are putting finishing touches on the rest of dinner. The women are plump and beautiful, with what I know as Afghani eyes—that translucent blue of ice and heat at the same time. Their hair can only be described as dark bronze. They take turns touching my skin and look at me with a bit of disbelief; I'm not sure why. They wear beautiful headscarves that have red thread and beads spiderwebbed around the edges, and each exudes an enormous sense of contentedness around her children, a wonderful exuberance of warmth. The children speak both Turkish and Kurdish and try to translate some of the Kurdish words into a Turkish that I will understand, but we always end up in peals of laughter. Even though we cannot communicate, we all seem to know what is being said.

A large tablecloth is placed in the centre of the living-room floor. An enormous platter is laid on top of it and soon one of the men brings in gigantic sheets of thin *lavash*, flatbread. Doug and Mesmut dump the roasted meat and vegetables onto the bread: chicken, lamb, eggplant, homegrown tomatoes and peppers with a bit of kick. The women have puréed the eggplants we roasted earlier, added some garlic and yogurt, and now serve it with spicy ground lamb on top. We all sit on the ground in a circle and pull the tablecloth over our feet and knees so as not to offend Allah (and to catch the crumbs). We dive in, scooping up the puréed eggplant with pieces of ripped *lavash*, stuffing ourselves with roasted meat and vegetables, washing it all down with *ayran*, a refreshing drink made of yogurt and fizzy water.

At the end of the meal, we all roll into bed. Doug and I are naturally forbidden to camp and are given space in the living room where we sleep soundly, startled only once in the middle of the night by a short burst of machine-gun fire somewhere in the hills.

We rise early, and before we can say good morning, breakfast has been prepared, the most wonderful breakfast I have ever seen: fresh bread, butter, sour cherry jam, honey, salty olives, peppers, tomatoes, hard-boiled eggs, the creamiest feta cheese imaginable, walnuts, and a yeasty, molasses-like spread made from grapes. Plenty of *chai* to go along with it, a nibble here, a nibble there until we cannot possibly put any more food into our stomachs. We look around at the culinary carnage we have left and a curious expression comes over Mesmut's face. "Douglas," he says, "I have a question for you."

"Mmmmhmm?" Doug replies sleepily, lying on the floor.

"In America, for breakfast, why do you eat these... ehm... potato chips and milk? I see this all the time on television and I think this must be awful." Doug and I giggle and don't even bother trying to explain it. Doug puts one last gorgeous walnut into his mouth and says, "Yup. It's pretty bad. Don't do it."

We all lie laughing on the floor, puffing our bellies up as much as we can, trying to see whose is the biggest. Two hours later, Doug and I say goodbye. We have difficulty mounting our bikes and more difficulty riding away, in part because we have made such good friends, in part because the food has immobilized us.

We manage to kick ourselves into high gear and continue riding on a high plateau past mounds of harvested hay and piles of bee hives stacked high in meadows. Occasionally we hear the cry of shepherds calling their sheep and see the snow-white peaks of Kurdish nomadic tents on the roadside or on river banks, like mini-mountains on the plain. In a devastating heat, we pedal our way up a ridge and near the top, tucked into a cirque, are more snow-white peaks of canvas. Sun-baked children in colourful wool clothes run about, clanging bells, trying to get all their sheep to stand in perfect lines that fan out from a circle of tents, like rays from a white star.

We begin a lengthy descent towards the Black Sea—three days of wonderfully treacherous plunges through narrow canyons where fruit trees grow on every patch of available soil. Children sit on the side of the road and sell their harvest of peaches, pears, and plums in beautiful handmade baskets. The canyon walls are high, but where the river's banks permit, makeshift greenhouses line the shore opposite us, accessible only by cable cars that seem too small to fit a whole person. Cases of tomatoes, peppers, and melons are stacked on the side of the road, ready to be picked up. We stop for a rest at a tea house, give a man some change, and he gives us an enormous bag filled with figs so fresh they look and taste like strawberries. We cannot possibly eat them all, but he will not let us leave with anything less.

We continue on past large towns built precariously on the sides of steep mountains, a thousand feet or more above the road, calls to prayer drifting down to us. On our last pass before the Black Sea, the humidity that has eluded us suddenly meets us head-on. The road climbs up, up, up through a steamy deciduous forest, past a handful of old Roman bridges draped in moss and grapevines. We crest the summit and switchback down towards the sea, rushing past terraces of tea in harvest, the occasional rooftop or minaret poking up through the foliage. Large burlap bags stuffed with tea leaves line the side of the road, and workers everywhere pause to wave and wipe sweat from their brows.

The Black Sea is a sight for weary eyes. It shimmers in the late afternoon sun and offers a cool breeze against the humidity. We strip down and dive in, letting gentle waves wash over our exhausted bodies.

After a while, I wander over to a small seaside tea plantation and ask the old woman there if we can camp next to it. She nods and as we set up our tent, she climbs into a large fig tree, where she whistles sharply and starts throwing fresh figs at us so fast we can't catch them all. She fills her skirt with more, clasps it together with one hand, and descends the tree. Over at our tent, she lets go of her skirt and a hundred and thirty seven figs roll around on the ground in front of it. She smiles and walks away. A few minutes later, she comes back with a large plate of baklava. The phyllo pastry is handmade, the butter is hand-churned, the pistachios are fresh-picked, and the honey comes straight from an apiary in town. No one should ever taste baklava unless it tastes like this: barely baked, more pistachio than pastry, soaked in just enough honey and a dash of rosewater, buttery, buttery, buttery. Doug and I lie on our backs in baklava coma after sharing one piece.

After the sun sets, we start to make dinner. Doug fires up the stove, and a man passing by on the beach looks at us and laughs. He returns a few moments later with an enormous propane stove borrowed from a restaurant a stone's throw away on the shore. One of the waiters from the restaurant comes with him, shows us how to light it, and tells us we can keep it until morning. He returns to the

restaurant and we hear faint music start to play; the wonderful combination of Arabic wailing and techno beat of popular Turkish music
drifts across the pebbled shore. The waiter climbs up onto the restaurant's roof, adjusting the loudspeakers so that they point our way. He
stays up on the roof, and when he sees that we have finished eating,
he switches the loudspeakers back to where they were, climbs back
down, and turns the music off.

We fall asleep to the sound of wind brushing through trees and
waves swirling through pebbles. A few hours later we are woken by
pulses of distant music and clapping and cheering that sounds like it
is coming from the restaurant. After an hour or so, Doug gets up and
goes outside to see what it's all about. He comes back a while later,
climbs into his sleeping bag, and lies stock-still without saying a
word. I wait ten minutes, then my curiosity gets the better of me.
"What was it?" I ask.

"A bellydancer... " he whispers, the awe of a child in his voice.
"A real, live bellydancer."

〜

I am not quite sure how to approach the subject of Turkish-
Armenian relations. It has been a dilemma, placing my experiences
in both countries in the same chapter. I do not wish to imply that
the countries are similar in any way. My reasons for writing about
the two countries together are simply that Turkey and Armenia occupy
adjacent areas, share a border (closed after the Turkish genocide of
Armenians that culminated in 1915, only recently re-opened and
even then, only at a singular, remote crossing), and were both part
of the cycling trip that Doug and I did from Istanbul through the
Caucasus to the Persian Gulf in 1998. The route we took was primar-
ily determined by the fact that the Turkish-Armenian border was
effectively closed, as are Armenia's borders with Azerbaijan. As a

result, the only way for us to visit Armenia and still finish in the Persian Gulf was to cycle from Turkey into Georgia and, three weeks later, cross into Armenia south of Tbilisi. We subsequently travelled across the country to the very bottom of a funnel-shaped piece of Armenian land nearly three weeks after that, the spout of which is shared with Iran, and from there we cycled on to the Persian Gulf.

I do not know enough about the Turkish genocide of Armenians to offer insight. I only know that when we told Turks we were going to Armenia, if it elicited any reaction at all, it was one of frustration, of "Why would you want to go there?" At no point did any Turk acknowledge the genocide, though for obvious reasons, it was not our place to question it and so we did not.

In Armenia, the reaction to our having been to Turkey was shrugged off, but the subject of the genocide always came up. Not in anger or fear but in a "just so you know about this part of our history" sort of way, in pain. The pain was so evident in people, in monuments, in discussion that it was difficult not to conclude that the genocide has formed a part of the present-day Armenian psyche. It appears to have instilled a silent nationalism, somewhat the same (though justifiably with more baggage) as Canadian nationalism in the face of the United States. Where the Canadian nationalism is based on an assumed inferiority complex and a need to protect ourselves from an overwhelming American influence, the Armenian one is based on a historical act of mass murder, where their country and its people were irrevocably changed by the hands of others. Figures vary, but it is known that between 1915 and 1923 more than one million Armenians were slaughtered by the Turks, and an equivalent number fled or were exiled. It is, therefore, impossible to write about Armenia without mentioning the genocide and the resultant stalemate with Turkey.

We enter Armenia from Georgia, where we have spent the past three weeks caught in a vortex of exhausting, aggressive friendliness, recipients of an intense pressure from the Georgians to be as proud of Georgia as they are. We are aware of Armenia's peacefulness immediately. At the border, the Georgian customs director is swaying drunk, while the Armenian one is reserved and offers us fresh sour cherries that he has picked just for us from a tree behind the trailer where he stamped our passports. The soldiers that man the crossing shake our hands in a formal and reserved manner and give us grapes; huge, yellow Armenian grapes that taste almost like melons. We buy a Fanta from a man at a roadside restaurant and after we chat with him for a while, he disappears into the restaurant and comes out again with the money we gave him, pressing the bills into Doug's hands.

We ride along a river valley, slowly climbing into Armenia's rocky landscape. Towns pop up here and there; stone houses with galvanized tin roofs and ornate spires and fences line the valley. Occasionally there is an outcropping of refurbished old rail cars that have been placed on the side of the road and turned into khorovatz restaurants, places that sell skewered, roasted meat. The aroma of it rouses our nearly-empty stomachs, but we cycle on and the road steepens to switchbacks. We climb and climb and climb up through grassy pastures where shepherds slowly walk their herds home. The light is golden, spreading a deep autumn glow. We have emerged from the valley onto a high alpine ridge void of any trees, houses, paths. The ridge is uniform and smooth, the road we ride on its only scar. The leaves on the trees below us are starting to turn colour, already a yellow so bright and deep it seems impossible.

Near the top of the pass, we see a series of small A-frame shacks and pull over to ask if we can spend the night there. We tell the woman there that we have a tent, but she leads us to one of the A-frames. She tells us that this is a restaurant and that the A-frames are eating rooms, where families or travellers can eat in private, but we can stay in one overnight because it's the quiet season now. We ask her if we can pay her anything, and she laughs and shakes her head.

"No, please," she says. "It's harvest time, so all of the farmworkers are staying here for free. They eat at eight o'clock, so if you would like some *khorovatz, chai,* vodka, watermelon, anything, just come."

Our intentions are good. We'll take a nap, we tell each other, and that way we'll be refreshed for dinner. Not a chance. We both wake the next morning, still fully clothed, having slept almost fourteen hours without stirring. Ravenous, but rested. Outside the sky is crisp, clear except for a solitary cloud that floats at eye level in the field across from us.

We find the woman who greeted us yesterday and she gives us green pears to take along, freshly picked. She cringes when we tell her we are going to Lake Sevan, then gives us more pears. "It's a big mountain you have to climb," she says. We set off, climbing past more sleepy villages covered in cabbage and sunflower fields, mounds of hay stacked so high next to the houses that they nearly conceal them. We descend into a small town and almost immediately begin to climb again.

As we are sitting by the side of the road having lunch, we see two men on donkeys coming down the hill towards us. As they pass they suddenly break into a loud argument. One rides away while the other gets off his donkey and pulls out a large knife. He dips it into his saddlebag and cuts us a large piece of fresh cheese, handing it over, still dripping with whey. He doesn't say a single word. Smiling, he bobs his head in farewell, then jabs his donkey in the belly with his heels and trots off to catch up with his partner. The cheese is delicious…creamy and salty, like feta.

We continue climbing. Just as we notice the path of the road switchbacking up another thousand feet or so, a car pulls up alongside us and the woman in the passenger seat reaches out with three gorgeous white peaches. The driver wipes his brow in sympathy with us, gives us the thumbs-up sign and they drive off. We lie on the ground and bite into the peaches, letting the juice drip into our mouths. Nearby, a woman selling fresh corn on the cob from a blackened cauldron of water heated by a raging fire laughs at us.

Lake Sevan is the pride and joy of Armenians, and when you approach it from the hunch of land to the north, after climbing all day, it is a sight of incredulous beauty. I crest the pass first and stop in my tracks. The green and yellow ridges that we have climbed up and down for the past few days are behind us. In front of me lies a lake, like a big lusty sapphire in a hollow, surrounded by desolate, craggy rock, high on one side, a plateau on the other. It stretches out beyond view, its southern end lost in the haze of sunshine and curvature of the earth. I grin so widely my teeth hurt, and when Doug pulls up behind me, he breaks into laughter so whole and heartful that I still remember it. We dance around on the abandoned road for a while, truly, genuinely happy to see this great Armenian sea.

Of course, one can also not mention Armenia without mentioning Ararat. Even though the mountain lies across the border in Turkey, it strikes me that it affects Armenians more than it does the Turks, strictly by geographic favour; Ararat lies on a desolate plain in Turkey but is visible from Yerevan, Armenia's capital, and is therefore part of one and a half million Armenians' daily landscapes. In Yerevan, Ararat's stunning, snowy peak hovers over the city like an unsuspecting cloud, its slopes hidden by Armenian smog. When I realize that I am not looking at a cloud, but that I am under the watchful eye of Ararat, I am humbled, and shrink as low to the ground as possible.

Doug and I ride into the face of Ararat, which becomes clearer and clearer as we leave the heavy air of Yerevan. Everywhere we stop, someone miraculously appears and gives us fresh fruit. We wind up

with so much that we start taking on the role too—we give everyone we pass some of our fruit: shepherds, farmhands, Armenian
travellers pulled off on the side of the road taking pictures of a
Turkish mountain.

We lunch in a field strung high with grapes. Off in the distance,
on a promontory that pokes the Turkish border, we see a monastery,
the site of Armenia's conversion to Christianity. Armenia was the first
Christian state, adopting the religion at the beginning of the fourth
century A.D. Its conversion from paganism is attributed to Gregory
the Illuminator, who reputedly tried to sell Armenia's king on
Christianity and was subsequently thrown into a deep, lightless pit.
The queen took pity on him and brought him food and water, keeping him alive for thirteen years. When the king fell ill, the queen
convinced Gregory to try to heal him, which he did. The king was so
grateful and impressed that he vowed to convert all of Armenia to
Christianity, and Armenia has subsequently been graced with several
monasteries, this one built overtop of the pit that housed Gregory. It
sits on a plain that leads to the base of majestic Ararat, the reputed
resting site of Noah's ark towering nearly 4600 metres above it, a
sight capable of converting even the most devout agnostic.

Doug and I pedal out to the promontory and climb down into
the pit where poor Gregory was kept. It is perhaps ten metres deep
and three metres wide, round, with stone walls and completely
eerie. No air, no light. Thirteen years.

For the rest of the day we hug the Turkish border, occasionally
spotting rusty, dilapidated watchtowers that look abandoned, but
which we are surprised to find are still in use. We ride through a
slew of towns where women sell strings of pears on the side of the
road. When we try to buy just one or two pears, the women won't
let us, so we buy a whole string, eight pears, attached to it by their
stems and hung neatly and alternately. The women marvel at our gear
as we try to fix the pears to the top of my rear panniers. We ride off,

dangling pears behind us like tin cans attached to a newlyweds' get-away car.

A few miles down the road, we enter a town crowded with watermelon vendors. Two of them, Armin and Varta, call us over and we ask them how far it is to the next town. "Oh, you don't want to go *there*," they say. "Stay here. Have some watermelon," Armin says, nodding his head at a pile of two hundred round, deep green melons beside him.

Varta picks one, slams it on the table they are sitting at, and cuts it into two halves, offering Doug and me a half each. We settle into the melon, smearing our cheeks with its thick, perfumy juice, spitting the seeds at passing cars. Armin and Varta boast about how hot this valley gets in the summer. "I heard it was fifty-five degrees this summer in Yerevan," says Doug. "Fifty-five!" they say. "That's nothing. Here it was sixty-five, easy." A man from a restaurant across the street brings us a tray of coffee and Fanta, shakes our hands, and returns to the other side of the road. Armin and Varta invite us to a *khorovatz* dinner, and we help them stash their melons, using an old Soviet motorcycle and sidecar. We fill the sidecar with melons, I sit on top, and Armin drives us to a small shack down the road where we unload them. Four or five trips later, the job is done.

Today is Armenian Independence Day, and a big feast has been prepared for seven or eight of us at the restaurant across the road from Armin and Varta's stand. A few of their friends join us, and we sit down at a table that heaves under the weight of food and drink. There is plenty of vodka, less Fanta, even less water ("There is water in vodka," says Armin, "have some"). There are plates of dried sausage, fresh tomatoes, fresh herbs, fresh peppers, feta cheese, butter cheese, three different kinds of bread, yogurt sauce and *khorovatz* after *khorovatz*: some lamb, some beef, some pork, and entire chickens' legs and thighs threaded onto skewers and roasted. There is also a very special kind of *khorovatz*—one of pork and fruit—and as I bite into it, all the juices run together. Complete and unadulterated heaven. I taste a slight tartness and ask Armin what it is. He points to a pomegranate and makes a squishing motion.

Everyone takes a bit of bread, with a bit of cheese or a chunk of meat or tomato, eats it, takes another chunk of bread and some herbs, eats that, picking and nibbling informally, washing it all down with vodka. In the background, a television blares and pictures of a parade and ceremonies in Yerevan flash across the screen. No one in the room seems interested that it is Independence Day, nor, frankly, do the people on the screen. I ask Varta if this is because the independence is relatively fresh. "No, not at all," says Varta. "It is because we've always been independent. We have always been our own people, and Armenia," he says, waving a skewer flamboyantly around his head, "has always been ours. We're not like the Georgians. We don't despise the Russians for having been here. We are Armenian and we are different from them, and Armenia belongs to us—the Russians know that."

We eat and eat and eat and then we all jam ourselves into Varta's Lada and zoom off down the road to a spring. It is a literal hole in the ground, where the spring comes up, a few feet from a lit-up garrison at the buffer zone between Turkey and Armenia. The hole seems bottomless—it is round enough to fit two or three people, so we take turns jumping in and cooling off. A few days ago, in the high alpine in the northern part of the country, it was cool enough to see frost at night, but here, at 10 in the evening on the plateau beneath Ararat, it must be over 30 degrees.

Doug and I wake early, still stuffed from the night before. We begin to climb a long, relentless pass right away. An hour later, Varta's black Lada careens past and pulls over on the side of the road in front of us. Armin and Varta stumble out of the car, hungover. They have come to tell us that we can't ride the pass, that we should stay with them for another day and eat watermelon. Doug and I look across the plain at Ararat and smile at each other. Armin pokes at the muscles in Doug's legs and looks at us exhaustedly. "Okay," they say, shaking our hands and promising to come and visit us in Canada. They climb back into the immaculate Lada and zip off back home, a blast of flamenco music booming through the windows. Within seconds we are wrapped in silence.

We spend the next few days climbing the ridges and folds of southern Armenia. It seems impossible to go anywhere without having to negotiate a mountain pass. The landscape becomes stonier and stonier and in the hills near the town of Djermuk, there is a view of sky and rock and sky and rock as far as the eye can see. It forces me to think about solitude and silence and strength. I look at it and I can feel Armenia's will, her character, her disaggregation.

We pass through towns where huge oak barrels are being scrubbed out for this year's wine harvest. At night, we camp under skies so clear that the stars feel like leaves on trees, close enough to touch. We coast along rivers, past small villages where people are

Karahundj is Armenia's Stonehenge, a series of ancient telescopes dating to 4200 B.C.

having *khorovatz* on the riverbanks and where, when we try to buy a
few apples, the vendor always throws in some peppers, apricots,
peaches, and cucumbers for free. We come to a place called
Karahundj, Armenia's Stonehenge, where an ancient outcropping of
tall, pointed rocks are arranged, on a height of land in the middle of
nowhere, in a pattern that once allowed someone to map stars. I cannot think of a more appropriate monument for Armenia.

Never before have I seen such vistas. Everywhere we are in this
country, we are in the middle of a vast landscape, whether on a
plateau 4600 metres under the peak of Ararat, or on Lake Sevan's
endless blue waters, or in the mountains of Djermuk, layer after layer
of rock unfolding in the distance. Nothing ever blocks the view,
nothing interrupts the path of the eye as it scans a stony, immense
horizon that spells thousands of years under the sun.

TURKISH & ARMENIAN RECIPES

Dockside Lahmacun

1 1/2 cups lukewarm water
a pinch of sugar
1 tsp. yeast
3 cups flour
a pinch of salt
1 tbsp. olive oil
2 tbsp. butter
1/2 tsp. sweet paprika
1 dried chili pepper, crushed
1 onion, minced
2 cloves garlic, chopped
1 tomato, minced
another pinch of sugar
1/2 lb. minced lamb
2 tbsp. tomato paste
a few handfuls of parsley and cilantro

Mix the water and sugar together in a large bowl. Sprinkle the yeast over top and let it sit for 10 minutes or so, until it begins to froth. Stir in the flour and knead until you have a smooth dough. Let the dough rest for 20 minutes or so, then knead in the salt and olive oil and set aside until the dough has doubled in volume, about an hour. In the meantime, melt the butter in a saucepan and add the paprika and chili. Cook for 1 minute over medium-high heat, until it becomes fragrant, then add the onion, garlic, tomato, and sugar. Cook for

3 to 4 minutes, until the onion starts to turn translucent. Add the lamb, toss well, and remove from the heat (the lamb will cook later in the oven). Heat the oven to 400°F. Divide the dough into four pieces and roll each out into a thin oval or round. Spread a bit of tomato paste on each one and then spread some of the lamb mixture over top. Bake in the oven on baking sheets for 8 to 10 minutes, so that the lamb is cooked, but the dough is still soft enough to roll up. Remove the lahmacun from the oven and let cool for a few minutes. Roll each of them up into a cone, stuff with sprigs of parsley and cilantro, and serve.

Serves 4 as a light lunch or snack.

Baklava

I've included a recipe for making your own phyllo pastry—it's a bit tricky, but it really does make a big difference in how the baklava tastes. Of course, you can substitute packaged phyllo instead. You can also substitute walnuts or almonds for the pistachios—all three nuts are used in baklava in Turkey. Authentic baklava is always soaked in honey, though, not sugar syrup, so use the best honey you can find.

2 1/2 cups flour
1/2 tsp. baking powder
1/4 tsp. salt
1 tsp. lemon juice
1/3 to 1/2 cup water
1/2 to 2/3 cup cornflour
1/3 cup butter
2 cups shelled pistachios, chopped
1 cup honey
1/3 cup water
1 tbsp. rose water

Mix the flour, baking powder, and salt together in a large bowl. Add the lemon juice and a quarter of the water. Keep adding the water while mixing the dough, until you have a soft dough. Knead for 5 minutes, until smooth, then cover with a damp cloth and let it rest at room temperature for an hour or so. Heat the oven to 375°F. Sprinkle a flat surface and rolling pin with some of the cornflour. Cut the dough into 8 or 10 equal pieces and roll each piece out into large rectangles until paper-thin. Sprinkle with more cornflour if the pastry sticks to the rolling pin or surface. Melt the butter in a saucepan over medium heat. Lightly brush a large baking sheet with some of the melted butter. Lay a piece of the pastry on the sheet, brush with butter, and lay another piece of pastry on top, brushing with butter again. Repeat until you have used half the sheets of pastry. Sprinkle the chopped pistachios evenly over top and place another sheet of pastry on top, brushing with butter. Repeat the layering and brushing with butter with the remaining sheets. Score the pastry into squares or diamonds and bake for 25 to 30 minutes, until lightly browned. In the meantime, put the honey, water, and rosewater in a saucepan and heat over medium heat, until the honey is thin. Pour the sauce over the baklava as soon as it comes out of the oven and let cool to room temperature. The honey will be absorbed. Store the baklava at room temperature, never in the fridge, where it will turn soggy.

Makes 8 squares, serving 8 as a dessert or as a snack.

Khorovatz Khozi Mis
(Pork *Khorovatz* with Fruit and Pomegranate)

This dish is a wonderful blending of the sweetness of fruit and fresh
pork with the tartness of pomegranate. Pomegranate molasses
is available at any ethnic or Middle Eastern food market.

2 lb. boneless pork loin, cut into large bite-sized chunks
2 pears, quartered
4 fresh figs, halved, or a handful of grapes
4 apricots, halved (dried or fresh)
2 tomatoes, cut into eighths
3 or 4 green onions, cut into 3-inch lengths
3 tbsp. oil
salt and pepper
pomegranate molasses

Heat a barbecue or broiler to medium-hot heat. Alternately
thread pieces of the pork, fruit, tomatoes, and green
onions onto metal skewers. Brush the khorovatz
with oil and sprinkle with salt and pepper.
Cook for 10 to 12 minutes, turning
occasionally so that all sides are
nicely browned. Brush with
pomegranate molasses and
cook for two more minutes.
Serve with rice, *pideh* or any other
kind of flatbread.

Makes 4 skewers, serving 4 as part of a meal.

Alexandre Dumas describes how to make *shashlik* (*khorovatz*):

You take a joint of mutton—the thick part of the leg if you can get it—cut it into pieces the size of a nut and let them soak for a quarter of an hour in a *marinade* of vinegar, onions, salt and pepper, while you prepare a bed of red-hot embers on the stove. Then you put your little bits of mutton on a wood or metal skewer and twirl it above the embers till the meat is cooked. It was, in fact, the nicest thing I had to eat during the whole of my travels in Russia. If the morsels of mutton could have stayed in the *marinade* overnight; if, when cooked, they could have been dusted with *sumac*, they would have tasted even better, but when one is pressed for time and there is no *sumac* ready to hand, such refinements are super-fluous. On occasion, when I had no skewer, I have often used my bayonet instead.

—*Adventures in Caucasia*

Ali Nazik Kebabi (Turkish Eggplant with Ground Lamb)

4 Japanese eggplants, or 1 large Italian eggplant
6 tbsp. olive oil
3 cloves garlic, minced
2 cups yogurt
1 1/2 tsp. salt
1 lb. ground lamb
1 tbsp. butter
1 tsp. dried red chili
1/2 tsp. pepper
a handful of fresh italian parsley, chopped

Heat the oven to 350°F. Cut the eggplants in half lengthwise and drizzle with 3 tablespoons of oil. Place eggplants on a greased baking sheet and roast, 15 to 20 minutes for small eggplants, about an hour for a large one. Remove the eggplants from the oven, let cool, and scrape the flesh away from the skin. Chop the flesh fine and fry it over medium heat with the remaining oil and garlic. Cook for 3 minutes, then stir in the yogurt and 1 teaspoon of the salt. Remove the eggplant from the heat and set aside. Fry the lamb in the butter over high heat, for 5 minutes, until the lamb is done. Drain and stir in the dried chili, remaining salt, and pepper. Spread the eggplant mixture over the bottom of a serving platter and heap the lamb in the middle. Sprinkle with parsley and serve. Great with flatbread!

Serves 4 as part of a meal.

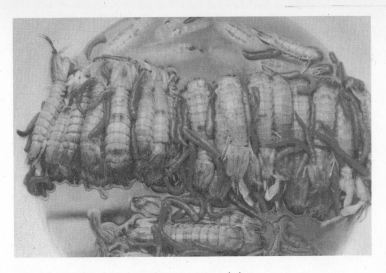

Crayfish and chilis for sale on the street in Bangkok

Buying bread from a father and son in the countryside near Poti, Georgia

Feudal stone towers near the Russian border in Svaneti, northern Georgia

Hawking strings of pears on the side of the road in Armenia

Roadside cantina near Tomatlán, deserted at sunrise

Crosses dot the roadsides in Mexico, marking where fatal accidents have occurred

Long, lonely roads near Bariloche, Patagonia

The "courtyards" of Bangkok—houses lining a klong in the middle of the city

Colourful foothills in northern Argentina, near the Bolivian border

The ancient pillars of Persepolis in Iran

A typical roadside restaurant in Busheer, Iran

A typical scene in Vancouver's Chinatown

The spectacular domes of the Blue Mosque in Istanbul

Watching the procession at a temple festival in Ubud, Bali

Mt. Bromo and the Sea of Sands in early morning light, Java

INDONESIA

An hour after sunset, on the eve of one of Bali's many temple festivals, a colourful crowd gathers in the centre of a village, seating themselves on a piece of well-trodden ground. They sit in front of a large white sheet drawn tightly across two bamboo poles, chatting, pulling excited children into their laps. A torch is planted behind the sheet and lit on fire, and the crowd hushes as, like the first raindrops of a torrential storm, small mallets are dropped onto the xylophones and drums of a gamelan orchestra. The children's eyes widen and fix on the screen. Suddenly the shadow of a puppet appears, gracefully moving its arms, its scratchy voice drifting through the audience. The shadow of another puppet emerges. In a flurry of heads and arms, the first puppet is threatened and recoils. Shadows of two more puppets appear, dashing about the screen, and an eight-and-a-half-hour story begins to unfold, told in ancient Javanese to an enthralled and spellbound audience.

These are the puppets of the *wayang*, or shadow puppet play. Although over two hundred puppets exist and more than thirty-five can appear in a single play, the puppets and their voices are controlled by one man. He sits behind the screen, cross-legged, next to the torch. Each puppet has its own character, voice, and spirit, its shadow as easily recognizable to Indonesians as movie stars are to westerners. The puppets are intricately decorated, painted with gold leaf and a cacophony of colours, which only the puppet master enjoys. The audience sees the puppets' shadows, their shapes brought to leaping heights and life by the flame behind the screen. Earlier in the day, I had watched a man making one of the puppets, and he painted it as if he were painting his own soul.

Understanding the *wayang* is the only way to understand Indonesia, the man told me. In the *wayang*, whose stories are loosely borrowed from East Indian Hindu-Buddhist epics, the left is in an endless struggle with the right; in life, on the screen, and in the story. The solution is not to have one side win over the other, but to find a balance. "In the West we want answers for everything," says Billy Kwan in *The Year of Living Dangerously*. "Everything is right or wrong, good or bad. But in the *wayang*, no such final conclusions exist."

My sister and I arrive in Bali separately but within minutes of each other. She has spent the summer planting trees in northern Ontario. Two days ago she was retrieving trees from snow caches and walking through walls of blackflies. When I find her standing outside of Denpasar's airport, she is staring up at the tall fronds of palm trees waving slightly under the weight of dense humidity, and I cannot fathom her shock. But the sparkle in her eyes tells me that this jolt to her system is a good one, one she has wanted to give it for quite some time. I, on the other hand, have not been in the western hemisphere for nine months and am nearing the end of my already-frayed absorption of culture. I have been in Southeast Asia for three months now and have become negligent in educating myself about places beforehand. In Asia, I have become lazy, finding it more interesting to hear about a country's culture and history from its own people, to contemplate and sift through the interpretations of events and let the most important ones rise, like cream in fresh milk, to the top.

Would it be wrong for me to say that we are here for no other reason than to see another culture and to give our western heads a good shaking up? Joanna, a student of art history and anthropology, has more of an idea of what she would like to see than I, and I am happy to hand myself over to her. We will spend a slow-paced month on Bali and in East Java, drinking everything in, letting the colours and language and light of these places saturate us so that they ooze outward through our pores. So we step from the airport into the orgy of the senses that is Asia.

As we dodge motorcycles, horse-drawn carriages, buses, cars, pushcarts, and waves of pedestrians in downtown Denpasar, we see a man deftly turning satays over coals in a food stall, fanning the flames with a stiff banana leaf. Fortunately, Joanna is as fearless an eater as I am, someone who habitually ignores sterile, western warnings about eating street food. We approach and ask for two or three satays each and the man laughs at us, white girls who think they know what they are ordering. We insist, and he hands us each a pandan leaf onto which he mounds steamed sticky rice and three browned sticks of meat. We sit on the curb and eat, amidst the brrraaahhhp! and beeping of motorcycles, the exhaust of minibuses, and straw dropped from mule-drawn wagons. An injured chicken wanders in and out of the traffic, eventually crushed into a pile of feathers and blood by tire after tire. Pedestrians squeeze by each other on the dirt sidewalk, laughing sharply and shouting over the street noise.

Our satays are delicious, and we give the thumbs-up signal to the cook, who grins at us. Halfway through eating them, Joanna suddenly stops and says, "What is this?"

"It's a satay," I tell her. "It's marinated meat, basted with... "

"I know what a satay is," she interrupts. "I mean what kind of meat is it?" We each take another bite. Definitely not chicken or pork. Certainly not beef, not on Hindu Bali.

We look over at the cook, who is still grinning at us. He nods, showing us his betel-stained teeth and points a curved, arthritic finger at a dog scampering into the traffic, trying to get at the pile of run-over feathers.

"Hmmm. A first for me." I take another bite and let it simmer on my tongue.

"Yeah. Pretty good too. Lean. Gamey…" she considers.

"Welcome to Asia," I say. She laughs, and we eat until there is not a grain of rice left on our pandan leaves and I know that the worst culture shock for her will be going home.

⌒

We leave Denpasar's tangle of traffic in a *bemo*, a small pick-up converted into a public transport vehicle. We sit in the back on benches among grinning Balinese and enormous bags filled with corn, betel leaves, and fragrant rambutan and durian fruit. Three live piglets lie on the floor, their legs hobbled to thick sticks that serve as handles so they can be carried like a satchel or small suitcase. The *bemo* winds its way slowly northward through the hills towards the town of Ubud, in the centre of the island. We pass glittering, glassy terraces of flooded fields, where farmers in straw hats stoop knee-deep in water and mud to plant rice seedlings. Pedestrians walk barefoot along the narrow paths that separate the terraces, balancing long, wobbling bamboo poles draped with baskets on their shoulders. The water in the rice fields reflects huge thunderheads forming in the sky, and the terraces stretch out to a distant, low cliff, where waves crash like rows of dominoes on a coast of volcanic dust.

We unload in Ubud and immediately decide to stay for at least a week. We are not yet sure why we feel compelled to do so, except for a mysterious, magical pull it already has on us, something that tells us there are things worth exploring here, in the town and beyond. As we are walking down a tranquil, colourful street, a small boy approaches us and asks us if we have a place to stay. He leads us to his family's home, where his mother offers us a small hut in the back for a very reasonable price. As we are unpacking, the boy knocks on our door and enters with a large basket filled with tiny finger bananas, pieces of fresh coconut and pineapple, lychee-like *salak* and tangelos. He teaches us the Indonesian words of the fruit—*pisang, kelapa, nanas, salak, jeruk*—and asks if we can exchange English and Indonesian words each afternoon, when he returns from school. Of course, we say, and he runs off.

In the mornings, before the heat settles in, Joanna and I borrow the family's bikes to visit some of the hundreds of temples that are scattered across the hills beyond town. We pass fresh-scrubbed children on their way to school who shout "Hel-LOH!" when they see us. We pass women who are placing tiny offerings of cooked rice, flowers, and fresh fruit in front of the shrines in appreciation of the good spirit, and to pacify the evil ones. We pass men wearing cloths carefully wrapped around their heads and ankle-length sarongs. They smile at us, always ask where we are going and always points us in the right direction. We pass other tourists, who hold their heads high and away from us in a dissociative manner, perhaps not wanting to be reminded that this island is filled with westerners looking for an Asian experience. And soon, we find ourselves getting up earlier and earlier in the mornings, heading straight for the rice paddies: me, for wandering and thinking, Joanna for exploring and sketching.

As we walk along the road, women washing clothes in milky streams or workers in the fields shout at us, encourage us to take short cuts through the rice paddies. They take our hands and lead us to more hidden shrines and temples than we ever thought possible. Bali, which is 100 kilometres long and 80 kilometres wide, is reputed to have more than eighty thousand temples, made of heavy, decoratively carved grey stone. Each temple seems appropriately placed, looming in its own most mystical spot. Old temples that have been buried by volcanic ash for centuries are uncovered with regularity, and in true Balinese spirit they are immediately put to use again, as though this rediscovered temple were a gift to the Balinese from the very gods worshipped in those temples.

In the afternoons, we meet with our young friend Wayan for Indonesian and English lessons. As we walk with him through the streets, he points to things and tells us their Indonesian names. We pause to snack on *srabi* (tiny crisp pancake cups with rice pudding and coconut), *pisang goreng* (fried bananas sold straight from the fire, all gooey and charred and good) or *jahe*, a hot ginger tea that puts a bit of life back into you after you've been walking all day. Wayan tells us that he is nine years old and was born and raised in Ubud. Joanna asks him what his favourite subject is in school, and he stops on the road, grabs a stick, and draws a map of Bali in the dirt. "Ah, geography," she says and he repeats it. He draws little circles all over his map of the island and shows us where the volcanoes are, then gives Joanna the stick and asks her to show him where she is from. She walks away from him, across the road, while Wayan furrows his brow and watches her as she draws an outline of Canada. He shakes his head, saying, "No, no—where do you live?" pointing to his sketch of Bali and looks curiously at us when we tell him that we don't live on the island. He looks around at the rice paddies and wavering palms. He sniffs the sweet, volcanic air, closes his eyes, and then opens them, looking at us. He laughs and shakes his head and we know we are fools for not living here.

Farther down the road I ask him what he wants to be when he gets older. "Indiana Jones!" he shouts, jumping up and down on his skinny, dusty legs. He laughs, then shakes his head again and twirls around and around, arms outstretched. He stops, reflecting for a moment, arms still stretched out, wiggling his fingers. He looks at us and says, "I want to be Balinese."

⌒

In the evenings, we eat in the local restaurants, which serve typically Indonesian fare: *gado gado*, a salad of fresh vegetables, tofu, boiled eggs, and bean sprouts topped with a dense, spicy peanut sauce and served with shrimp crackers (*kerupuk*, which look like styrofoam chips but taste delicious and which have a wonderful habit of clinging to your tongue, as if hanging on for dear life); *nasi goreng* or *mee goreng*, a rice or noodle dish, fried with chicken, shrimp, and a healthy dose of chili peppers, served with cucumbers to cool the palate; or a Balinese special, *bubur injin*, a pudding of shaved coconut and black rice that is delicious, but is so rich that Joanna can't face it more than once on the whole trip.

After our dinners, when we walk back to our hut through dirt streets deserted except for the occasional scavenging dog, the murmurs of Balinese singing or chanting in their homes drift out to meet us. Along darkened *kampungs*, the glow of lanterns or hurricane lamps from their houses lights our way and we hear children laughing as they fall asleep amidst the long, eerie squawks and groans of bamboo. In this serenity in the centre of Bali, it is easy to forget that we are in one of the most crowded places on earth, the eye of the hurricane that is Indonesia.

On our third morning in Ubud, we are walking through the rice terraces when a young farmer shouts at us and trots through the field to meet us. "Please," he says breathlessly, "there is a temple festival in my village this afternoon. You are welcome." He smiles and bows slightly, then gives us directions to his village, turns, and runs back into the field.

Temple festivals on Bali are quite common and take place in communities at least once during the 210-day Balinese year, on the lunar birthday of each temple in that community. Most communities have two or three temples, so that makes over a hundred thousand festivals for one Roman year on Bali, which means that on any given day, there are about forty temple festivals going on somewhere on the island, in addition to everyday celebrations like weddings, funerals, and other rites of passage, which are also very public affairs.

That afternoon, we are called to the festival by a loud thumping from one of the temple's drum towers. Joanna and I make our way along the paths through the terraces to the village and arrive just in time. As guests, we are permitted to take part in the events, but since this is our first temple festival, we simply observe, out of respect for the villagers and their religion. In Bali, spirits are seen everywhere and in everything, and the festivals occur on days when the gods and spirits are believed to descend from heaven to enjoy the offerings presented to them by their worshippers.

The dirt road to the temple is packed with a procession of villagers. Against a backdrop of lush green palms and rice terraces, the unmarried women of the village walk first, empty handed, dressed in ornate gold sarongs and tight, batiked blouses. The married women follow, wearing crowns of pungent frangipani flowers on their heads and a few grains of rice pasted to the middle of their foreheads. They balance large bowls of offerings on their heads; layers of fruit and rice and whole roasted ducks are decoratively piled into cones a metre high. The flowers and fruit are so perfectly ripe that their perfumes float seductively through the air. The men follow behind, dressed in white smocks, yellow sarongs, and colourful head coverings.

As the women enter the temple, they are blessed by the priest, who calls on the gods to descend and partake in the celebration. While the priest chants and waves incense, our attention is drawn outside, where the men gather for a cockfight. "This is a way for the men to settle small conflicts and relieve the tension that exists within their communities," one of the villagers tells us. The cocks charge at each other, the men cheer, blood is shed, and money passes hands.

As the sun sets, the smell of satays fills the air, and we see that an area has been cleared for less religious festivities…a virtual carnival is in full swing, with booths selling clothing and trinkets and local delicacies. Joanna and I snack on *kueh kacang hijau* (sweet mung bean sprout cakes), a wonderful union of crunch and custard. Fire-eaters roam while gulping flames, gamelan orchestras plink and plunk away, their notes hanging in the heavy, scented air, men slap cards on tables, and children gather for an eight-hour shadow puppet play. We see the man from the rice field who invited us here, and he approaches us with a smile, then motions for us to look around the corner. In a clearing, bare-chested men sport sarongs and sharply carved and painted masks, crouching and stepping through the elaborate *topeng* dance. Inside the temple, the women gracefully sway through their *pendet* dance, each perfected, minute movement an offering to the gods and spirits.

At dawn, at the end of it all, the women carefully pack up their offerings, placing them inside covered baskets so that the gods will not see them, and trudge home, weary children in tow. For the next couple of days, they will serve the offerings in their homes as thanks to the spirits who provide them with such a rich and peaceful existence.

~

A low moaning gradually fills the pre-dawn air, like a siren in the distance. The moan, lamentful, gets louder, stronger, wailing now, and I open my eyes to orient myself. I am lying on a bed, in the dark, Joanna on the bed beside me. The room is pitch black, save for a corner where slats of light from a streetlamp slip through a shutter, beaming onto the floor and walls. The wail, a single voice, is quite loud now and when the voice pauses for breath I can hear quite clearly the crackle of a loudspeaker. I glance at my watch: 4:30 a.m. The wail peaks and, five minutes after slipping so surreptitiously into the air, it abruptly stops. The loudspeaker crackles again for a

Aspiring superheros near Borobudur

moment and then it too is silenced. Bugs creak and a car rumbles slowly by on the dirt road outside our door. And then gradually, the shuffling of many feet, the opening of many windows and doors, the starting of an engine here and there, a mother's words to her son as she pushes him outside... within half an hour the town is awake, slowly gathering itself for another day, caressed into consciousness by a call to worship Allah.

We are on Java, where Islam is the predominant religion. Java is busy, crowded, even in the most remote of spots, imbued with a sense of purpose, direction, accomplishment. Everywhere everyone is doing something, going somewhere, working—hard. And five times a day the wail that I have never heard until reaching Java floats through the air, encouraging briefly emptied streets and filled mosques.

On a train heading towards the centre of the island, we are inundated with food. We are travelling in third class, sharing worn wooden bench seats with a dozen live chickens tied together by their feet into one bunch. Small, happy children in RoboCop T-shirts climb all over us, offering us handfuls of peanuts, endless questions streaming from their mouths. Their mothers watch us and offer oranges and salak. They are on their way to Surabaya, on the east coast of Java, to visit family. There are eight children between them, and it is impossible to tell which mother has which children. Each behaves as though they are all her own, in a caring, unpossessive way. Nor is there division in the children, who treat their friends and cousins as siblings.

An hour into the train ride, the women open a large basket and pull out an enormous tin of cooked rice with chilis and tempeh, a savoury cake made of fermented, pressed soybeans. A sash of brilliantly coloured fabric that held the tin and its lid together is unravelled and spread on the floor of the train as a tablecloth. The children and their mothers pull us over to their feast, handing us small pieces of banana leaves to scoop the food into our mouths. They motion for us to cover our feet with the cloth so as not to offend Allah. The children press pieces of tempeh into our mouths and watch as we chew, our teeth releasing a wonderful nutty flavour from the soybeans.

At each stop hordes of people board the train with goods to sell: sticky rice tubes called lemper, wrapped like Christmas crackers in pandan leaves; deep-fried tofu, or tahu; fresh-cut nanas; fuzzy rambutans that look like the nose of a Muppet; packaged kerupuk; still-sizzling pisang goreng. The vendors rush through the train and shout,

"*Nasi, nasi, nasi, nasi, nasi, nasi*…" in unrelenting voices over the noise of settling passengers. Hungry people grab the vendor's arms or the rattan baskets that the food is piled in, and with a deft, swift movement that involves no speech or eye contact, money and food are exchanged. The vendors stay on the train until the very last minute, jumping off as the locomotive picks up speed, staggering to stable ground and walking back to the platform to wait for the next train.

A few hours later, at Probolinggo, we say goodbye to the children and wish their mothers a safe journey, Allah be praised. We step off the train and head into the hills. The valleys become narrower, the rice terraces have disappeared and here, on the steepest of mountainsides, crops of onions, cabbage, and carrots are grown, with field workers precariously balanced on the slopesides all day. We approach a line of volcanoes that stretches across Java and at Mount Bromo, about fifty kilometres inland from Probolinggo, we have a landscape before us like no other.

We climb to the rim of a crater and look over the edge only to see the crater of Mount Bromo nestled within this larger one, about five miles away. Between it and us is a vast, undulating sea of sand. Pleats of desolate land stretch up the smaller crater, from which a plume of steam rises, like a constant smoke signal. We descend into the outer crater and walk through a flat of volcanic sand for a couple of hours to Mount Bromo in cool, clear mountain air. For the first time in Indonesia, we see no one. We turn, and we look, and we enjoy the silent, humbling landscape, our footsteps the only noise for hours. We reach the inner rim and walk around its narrow edge. Under the thin crust of hardened lava that covers its heart, we hear hissing and bubbling, its steam a reminder of how vulnerable we are. A long, thick cloudbank pours over the edge of the outer rim and approaches us quickly, enveloping the peaks around us. As we descend Mount Bromo, we realize that we still have not seen anyone for almost five hours now. Then, slowly, off in the distance at the edge of the horizon of sand, a shimmering smudge appears and grows larger, into a figure, then into two, then into four.

Two men smile and wave at us as they approach. Their two mules, piled high with baskets and fabric, trudge behind them. The baskets  are filled with cabbages and the mules look exhausted. They stop walking as we pass them. The men look around, up at the blanket of cloud overhead, and untie one of the saddlebags on their mules. They call us over and hand us parcels of *lemper*, tie the saddlebag up again, and keep on walking. We unravel the pandan leaves and are left with a sticky tube of rice, stuffed with chicken and chilis, warming our insides as the sun sets behind the surrounding peaks. We lose sight of the men quickly; by the time we reach the lip of the rim a shadowy haze clings to everything, and we realize we are walking through a layer of clouds that separates us from brightening stars. The clouds sink and rise eerily, surrounding us, and for at least the fifth time today we realize that we are in a unique and special place.

⁓

Three or four days later, after slowly winding our way down from the hills, we arrive in Yogyakarta, Indonesia's second largest city. We are once again surrounded by rice paddies and roads packed with all types of transportation, from donkeys and carts to state-of-the-art air-conditioned mega buses, from *becaks*, or bicycle taxis, to shiny-new Land Rovers.

Joanna and I spend a day at Prambanan, a site of ninth-century Hindu temples that rise as steeply from the plain as the volcanoes just outside of town. It is a breathtaking sight, and we explore from dawn until dusk, clambering up and down temple steps, sketching the ornate stonework and simply sitting halfway up the temples, staring out onto the plain rife with beeping traffic, on the edge of the *kampungs* of Yogya. Eventually, the site shuts its gates, and we make our way slowly and reluctantly back into town.

On the main strip of Yogya, vendors sell anything and everything. They spread their wares out on the sidewalk—used combs, shoe polish, press cards, bootleg tapes, T-shirts, broken sandals—and will consider any price offered. Once the sun has set, the food carts emerge and Yogyans can walk and eat for miles and miles.

As we squeeze our way between pedestrians and hissing and sizzling food carts on Pawirotaman Street, we are hungry, but I have a rule: You don't eat the first thing you see when you stumble across a street like this. In the midst of such abundance and choice, we will not starve tonight, so we let our stomachs grumble until we find exactly what we want, which is simply something new, something we have not yet seen or tasted in Indonesia. We walk down the street, lit by the food carts' lanterns, through clouds of fragrant smoke. Everyone is laughing and smiling, chatting with the vendors they know, buying a little something to get them home. Beside some of the carts, between all of the pedestrians and *becaks* and stamping donkeys, mats laid out for customers are full of small, taut men with wide smiles shovelling rice and satays and curries into their mouths. The noise is incessant—the hissing of gas flames, the banging of metal spoons on woks, shouting, slurping—and we can't decide what to have. A driver motions to us and tells us to sit in his *becak*. He drives us slowly down the street, past more and more carts and mats and fragrant sizzles to a small *kampung* just off the street. He points to a small *warung*, where everyone inside is sitting cross-legged on the floor, completely absorbed in their food. The smell from this tiny place is glorious, tropical and steamy, of coconut and fruit and rice.

As we enter the *warung*, the driver sticks his head in and shouts something at the woman who owns the place. She nods and motions for us to sit down. She immediately brings some *jahe* and a few moments later places two platters in front of us one with rice and the other with a yellow mass of fruit and chicken in sauce, topped with the omnipresent Indonesian garnish—boiled eggs and chopped cilantro. The fruit is stringy but smooth, and its silky texture reminds me of the milkweed pods we used to open at our cottage and pluck apart in the wind. It slides down our throats, sweetened further by the coconut milk it swims in. "Do you like it?" the woman asks. We nod. "It is only made in Yogya," she says "We call it *gudeg*."

"What's the fruit?" I ask, and she disappears, returning a few moments later with a huge, spiny, grey-green fruit the size of a giant's football. "*Nangka*," she says, what we know as jackfruit, an inoffensive look-alike of the pungent, smaller durian. To make this dish, she uses slightly unripened *nangka*, which bounces back in the mouth. As we eat, she tells me what I will need to make *gudeg*; kaffir leaves, fish sauce, candlenuts, galangal. The measurements I will have to figure out for myself, she tells me, because she has done it so often that she has forgotten what they are. She does it by feel now, and this is the way it should be done, she says.

We wander back to our hotel as the food stalls are packing up. The street is still busy, but no one is hungry any more. It is time to sleep. Even the roosters in the wooden cages that are hoisted on poles of varying heights in the courtyard of our guest house are covered and quiet.

In the morning we head to Borobudur, a ninth-century Buddhist monument, as significant as Cambodia's Angkor Wat. As we approach the site, our jaws drop. It is massive, the Buddhist representation of the cosmos, carved out of stone in nine layers, taking one from earth, or the world as we know it, to nirvana. Its walls house over fifteen hundred intricately detailed bas-reliefs that depict, as Michael Palin put it, "the Buddhists' journey to enlightenment, complete with setbacks and seductions." To experience it properly, one must walk around each layer, following the story carved into Borobudur's walls all the way to the top, to the layers of nothingness and nirvana.

This is Joanna's reason for coming here, the one thing she wanted to see. She spends the day absorbed in her black book, sketching. This, like the rest of Indonesia, is beyond anything we'd ever expected. As we walk slowly up and around the nine layers of Borobudur towards nirvana, I find strands of jackfruit between my teeth and suck on them, each one a jolt of flavour from the night before. At the end of the day, we sit at the top among serene, larger-than-life stone Buddhas and watch the sun setting on Java's rice fields. The sun lowers itself through the haze onto a green ridge scattered with old volcanic cones. It morphs into a ball of pure vermilion, sinking past a strip of cloud that breaks it into two flaming segments before it disappears altogether. All this as a peaceful stone Buddha watches it set before us. There cannot be any other place like this on earth.

⌇

I think of how well the puppets of the *wayang* represent the people of Indonesia. This figure, carefully carved out of a thin, flat piece of leather and delicately attached to slender sticks that give it life, performs in a way that is simultaneously modest and larger than life. To me, it is a reminder of Indonesians…calm, friendly, soulful…whose traits are reflected more powerfully in their shadows, or in the memories of a trip, than in their immediate selves, moving from two-dimensional to three in contemplation, through spirit and generosity.

INDONESIAN RECIPES

Bubur Injin (Balinese Black Rice Pudding)

This dish is quite rich, and just a small amount is enough to satisfy any craving. White and black sticky rices and palm sugar are available at any Asian food market.

1 cup white Thai sticky rice, soaked overnight
1 cup black Thai rice, soaked overnight
1/4 cup palm sugar or brown sugar
a pinch of salt
2 cups coconut milk
a handful of shredded coconut

Line a sieve or steamer with a clean dishtowel or cheesecloth and place the soaked rice in it. Fill a pot or the bottom of a double boiler with water and place the sieve or steamer over top, making sure that it doesn't touch the water. Cover, bring to a boil, and steam for 30 minutes, stirring once. Check it occasionally to make sure the water hasn't evaporated from the bottom of the pot. In the meantime, place the palm sugar, salt, and coconut milk in a saucepan and bring to a boil over medium-low heat. Stir occasionally, and once the sugar has dissolved, reduce the heat to low. When the rice is tender, place it in a bowl and pour the coconut mixture over top. Stir until well combined, and set aside at room temperature to let it cool. The longer it sits, the more coconut milk it will absorb, and the softer the rice will be. The Balinese generally let it sit for 2 to 3 hours. Just before serving, toast some shredded coconut in a small frying pan over medium-high heat until nicely browned. Sprinkle it over top of the pudding and serve.

Serves 4 for dessert.

Coconut *Sambal*

In Indonesia, *sambals* are served on the side, with all dishes. They are usually made with chilis, and this one is wonderful with any curry, or as an alternative to the peanut dressing of the *gado gado*. Fresh coconut is best, but dried can be used.

1 cup freshly grated coconut, or 1 cup dried, tossed in
   1/4 cup water and set aside for 20 minutes
1 red chili, seeded and minced
juice of 1 lime
a pinch of salt
1/2 small onion, minced

Toss all the ingredients together and chill for an hour or two, or even overnight, to allow the flavours to emerge.

Makes about 1 1/2 cups, serving 4 as a condiment.

Gado Gado

This dish is everywhere in Indonesia, and for good reason. It has the quintessential elements of Indonesian cuisine: a balance of sweet and sour, smooth and crunchy, spice and cool freshness. *Kerupuk* are available at any Asian food market.

1 tbsp. oil
1 clove garlic, minced
2 shallots, minced
juice of 1 lime
1 chili, fresh or dried
1 tbsp. soy sauce
1 tsp. brown sugar
1/4 cup finely ground peanuts
1/2 cup coconut milk
1/2 cup water
1/2 tsp. salt
a handful of peanuts, chopped
1 small green cabbage, shredded
2 carrots, sliced
1/2 lb. green beans, trimmed
3 potatoes, sliced or cut into chunks
1 small cauliflower, cut into florets
1/2 cucumber, peeled and sliced
2 cups bean sprouts
2 hard-boiled eggs, cut into wedges
kerupuk, or shrimp crackers

Put the oil, garlic, shallots, lime juice, chili, soy, sugar, peanuts, coconut milk, water, salt, and peanuts into a saucepan and bring to a boil over medium-low heat. Cook for

8 to 10 minutes, until thickened. Remove the sauce from heat, and set aside to cool. In a large pot of boiling water, cook the cabbage, carrots, green beans, potatoes, and cauliflower in separate batches until tender. When each batch is finished, drain it and place it in cold water. Drain again and arrange the vegetables on a serving plate. Garnish with cucumber, bean sprouts, and hard-boiled eggs. Pour the cooled sauce over top and spread the *kerupuk* around the edges of the plate.

Serves 4 for lunch or a light dinner.

Gudeg

This dish is a specialty of Yogyakarta, the cultural centre of Java. Jackfruit, canned or fresh, should be available at any Asian food market, as should turmeric root, galangal (a cousin of ginger), kaffir lime leaves, fish sauce, and candlenuts. The measurements are guidelines. It's best to adjust the seasonings to your taste—make it your own.

2 tbsp. oil
8 chicken pieces (thighs and legs work best)
salt
pepper
8 shallots
3 cloves garlic
1 inch turmeric root, peeled and chopped
    or 1/2 tsp. ground turmeric
2 tsp. fish sauce
4 candlenuts, or macadamia nuts, or skinned almonds
1/2 inch piece of galangal, chopped, or the same
    amount of gingerroot
2 chilis, chopped
1 tbsp. coriander seeds
2 kaffir lime leaves
3 cups coconut milk
juice of 1 lime
1 lb. underripe jackfruit, peeled and sliced, or 1 lb. tinned
    jackfruit, drained and rinsed
a handful of cilantro, chopped

Heat the oil in a large pot over high heat. Sprinkle the chicken pieces with salt and pepper and cook them in the pot until browned on both sides. Remove the chicken from the heat and set aside. Combine the shallots, garlic, turmeric, fish sauce, candlenuts, galangal, chilis and coriander in a food processor or mortar and pestle and blend until you have a paste. In the same pot that you fried the chicken in, add the paste and fry it over medium-high heat for 2 to 3 minutes. Add the chicken, kaffir lime leaves, coconut milk, and lime juice and bring to a boil. Reduce the heat to medium low and cook for about 30 minutes, stirring occasionally. Add the jackfruit, and cook for a further 15 minutes, until the sauce has thickened. Serve sprinkled with chopped cilantro and plain rice.

Serves 4 for dinner.

Lemper

These tubes of rice are wonderful travelling food. If you can't find pandan or banana leaves (which should be available at any ethnic food market), substitute aluminum foil. Some of the flavour will be lost, but the essence will still be there.

1 cup sticky rice
3 cups water
1 cup coconut milk
a pinch of salt
4 9-inch squares of pandan leaves, banana leaves,
   or aluminum foil
1 skinless, boneless chicken breast, cooked and shredded
1 red chili, chopped

Soak the rice in 2 cups of water for 15 minutes. Drain and rinse it, then place it in a saucepan with the remaining cup of water, the coconut milk, and salt. Bring the mixture to a boil over medium heat, cover and reduce the heat to low. Cook for 15 minutes, until all the liquid has been absorbed. Remove from the heat and let cool until you can handle it with your hands. Place a few tablespoons of some of the rice on one of the leaves. Spread some of the chicken and chopped chili on top and cover with more rice. Tuck in the sides of the banana leaf and roll the rice up in it, so that none of the rice is showing. Repeat with the remaining ingredients. Toast on the barbecue for 2 to 3 minutes on each side, or place under a broiler until the leaves are slightly charred, about 2 minutes on each side. These are eaten at room temperature in Indonesia, but are just as delicious warm.

Makes 4 rolls, serving 4 as a snack.

NORTHERN
ARGENTINA

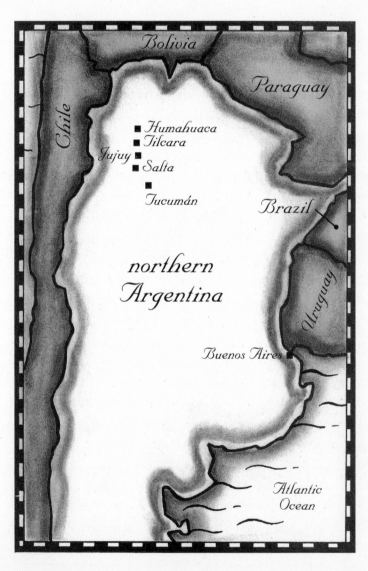

From a height of land off Argentine National Ruta 9, I look north along a string of ruby-coloured Andean foothills. If I hopped on my bike and followed them for a day, they would take me to the Bolivian border, high up onto the *altiplano*. I am already at 12,000 feet, beside the spine of South America, and I feel as though I have entered a different layer of the atmosphere. Colour is punched up, saturated, with a penetrating depth. Any shade of blue becomes azure in its purest form. The red of the mountains, which would seem a dusty, dull red at sea level, is suddenly pushed, as though it were being digitally altered, into realms of brilliant crimson. The landscape takes on a clarity that makes the slopes of mountains jump out so much they seem unreal, like an artist's three-dimensional interpretation, something I could grab with both hands, and plunk down somewhere else. Clouds seem to hover just inches overhead, and when I reach up to touch them, my weatherbeaten hand shields me from explosions of white vapour. I feel as though I am being pulled into it, the white equivalent of a black hole.

I am here because the landscape intrigues me, because I wanted to peer around the bends in the Andean spine. I have unexpectedly found myself washed in colour. Gusts of hot air swirl around me, the only noise I have heard all day. In the distance, I think I hear the clang of a goat's bell or the tinkle of a wind chime, but it seems impossible that anything could survive here. I sit on a hill overlooking an empty canyon and the road that runs through it, dwarfed by 20,000-foot peaks. The longer I stare, the more I see evidence of life, hidden by the vibrant colours of this landscape: a tiny village due east, a few kilometres away, whose flat-roofed mud-brick houses blend into a swath of brown clay; a small white church in a clump of trees above me; a young boy kicking up some dirt as he descends one of the foothills; an old woman placing something in a round clay oven outside her adobe-type home. A few minutes later a gust of wind brings the smells of dust and baking dough. The boy passes, waving at me and whistling to himself, trotting towards the village. I watch until I lose sight of him, the canyon swallowing him in its reds and browns and ribbons of green.

Farther down the highway, I come to the streets of Humahuaca: wide cobblestone alleys flanked on either side by long blocks of mud-brick walls. Doors and windows are sunk into the walls, occasionally lying open to reveal a person's life inside, in a beautiful courtyard or a dim, dusty sitting room. The doors and windows are Humahuaca's most notable characteristic and for days I wander around, staring at them, sometimes sitting in front of them for hours, studying their intricacies. Some are made of cactus wood, taken from the enormous, ancient cacti that are scattered through the foothills. Tiny pockmarks dot the wood where thorns once were. Other doors are decorated with delicate, swirling wrought iron and yet others are long, thin, vibrantly painted boards that remind me of balcony doors in a certain quarter of Paris.

The town of Humahuaca is not very big, and yet I manage to get lost. Though the doors are different, the streets themselves all look the same, complicated by the fact that identical sets of children always seem to be playing on each corner or running past me in the street. One group of them senses that I have been walking around in circles. They shout at me in Quechua, the native language here, and run ahead of me, leading me through the maze of walls and streets to the main square. They continue on, down a road by a wide river bed that has been cracked in the desert sun. They bring me to a market where women in bright woven shawls and bowler hats sell vegetables and clay cooking pots. The children disappear in the crowd as I wander through, past sacks and bushels filled with locally grown squash, with dried beans and with quinoa, a tiny, nutty grain that unravels itself into a curlicue when cooked. I pass a woman who is selling potatoes with skins the colour of violets, the surface of which looks as though they have had gold dust breathed on them by an Incan king. The woman slices one in half for me, revealing a creamy yellow inside. The woman next to her cuts open one of her own and shows me its deep purple flesh. They look at each other and shrug. One of them says to me, "*Es la vida*," that's life.

At the end of the day, the women pack up, climb into crowded tiny buses and head north, back to their villages until next week. I am camped on the other side of the evaporated river, and as I cook myself some of the purple potatoes for dinner, I see the children making their way over the river bed towards me. They have brought some sticks and a soccer ball and set up a game in front of my tent. They whack the ball with their sticks, a game somewhere between hockey and soccer. No rules or teams seem to exist, but each child seems to know exactly where his or her loyalty lies. They have told me I can't play because I'm bigger than they are, but I can watch. A few of them appropriate my bike and ride around in circles on the river bed while I eat my potatoes, succulent and delicious, with a heavier texture than the potatoes I am used to, as if I can taste the richness of the earth they grew in. The kids play until it is dark, when suddenly the gusting wind dies and all that can be heard are the faint echoes of a town closing up for the evening, the banging of doors, the squawk of chickens, the laughter of men at the end of their day.

I ride south down a wide valley of polychrome sand to the town of Tilcara. From the road, I can see a massive site of stone fortifications, the pre-Columbian ruins of El Pucará. I set up camp nearby and climb the steep hill up into town. I sit in the main square, watching pre-siesta goings-on. Children are busy buying fruit slushes shaved from a huge block of melting ice, and an old man has given them all balloons, for no apparent reason. Everyone is dressed up in freshly pressed black and white clothes.

I spend the afternoon in the ruins, which are manned by a guard who tells me there is a wedding in town and he has to leave but I should feel free to wander through the ruins and explore wherever I want. El Pucará is set on a hill spattered with twenty-foot-high cacti overlooking Tilcara. A series of waist-high walls and adobe buildings have been made from thin, layered set stone; it stretches over the entire hillside. I have the place to myself and watch the guard slowly pick his way over scorched cobblestone into town. It is silent, its streets abandoned in the midday heat. A hot wind has spent the morning gathering and now spills down the valley violently, kicking up mini tornadoes of sand and multicoloured dust.

The town is deserted as I make my way back through it, not even a dog scrounging for food or panting in the spindly shade of a cactus. My walk has made me hungry. I stroll down a lane and hear some voices coming from a small restaurant; its sign is propped out on the street, advertising locro, a local stew of beans, squash, and beef. Its door is wide open.

I walk in and hear a big cheer in the distance. The restaurant is completely empty except for a man sitting at the bar. He has his head on the counter, asleep. I hear some faint, tinny music and voices in the back, so I walk past the bar, around a dark corner and into a courtyard, suddenly blinded by sunlight.

I hear a pin drop. I blink. I stand, sunburned, weatherbeaten, dusty in my cycling clothes before a group of two hundred stunning, Brylcreemed, lipsticked, every-hair-in-place individuals seated at an enormous table. I blink again. Directly in front of me sit a woman and a man, he in a tuxedo, she in a sequined white bodice and flowing skirts, a tiara placed delicately upon her perfect head. Ah. The wedding.

"*Hola*," I say, and the group lets out a wild cheer. I am grabbed and shoved down the length of the table where there is an empty seat and am plonked down into it. Someone snaps a napkin open and drags it across my lap, another person hands me a glass filled with wine. All two hundred guests hoist their glasses and we toast the bride and groom.

The first course has already been served, but, the old woman sitting next to me tells me, I didn't miss anything. The cheese wasn't old enough, she says and shakes her head, wondering if I will commiserate. The courtyard is raucous. Everyone shouts up and down the table. The children run from one tickling uncle to another, shrieking with excitement. I see the guard from El Pucará and he waves cheerfully at me. Two men sitting across from me recognize me from the road; they passed me this morning on their way into town, they say. The second course arrives and wine glasses are refilled. We all stare into the shallow bowl that has been placed in front of us.

"No... *no es posible*," the old woman next to me mutters. It can't be. She looks up at the man across from her. "*¿Locro?*" she asks with a sneer. He laughs and nods. "*El mejor locro del mundo*," he says, winking at me. The best *locro* in the world.

The old woman grimaces and looks around her. Everyone else has tucked in without hesitation. She reluctantly picks up her spoon and drags it through the stew. I take a bite and taste a purée of slightly sweet, spicy squash. White beans give it a definition beyond plain soup; chunks of beef lend a heavier texture that pushes warmth and comfort through my bones, even in the searing heat.

The man across from me tells me that *locro* is a peasant dish that wouldn't normally be served at a wedding, but this is Tilcara, and the man who makes the best *locro* in the world lives here. The groom grew up here and then moved to Buenos Aires, but when he came back to get married, he knew he had to have *locro* at his wedding, as a reminder of his roots.

I look around the table. Every dish is empty and each and every guest has a smile in his or her eyes. Even the old woman beside me is licking the tail end of the stew from her spoon. She places it firmly back on the table, dabs her lips with her napkin and avoids our eyes. Finally she looks over at us, shrugs, and says, "*Bueno, bueno. Okey?*" The man across from her laughs and says that he has never heard her admit that she was wrong before.

The feast continues for hours; plate after plate of beef, grilled, boiled, stewed, raw, jug after jug of wine. The table is a disaster: spilled drink, a thousand dirtied glasses and plates. The catering staff has long since joined us in the celebration and we receive the food sporadically. We have given up asking for wine hours ago. A mess of bottles have been placed on the table and we serve ourselves. To finish the meal, someone has rummaged through the kitchen and found a few chunks of hard, Parmesan-like cheese and a block of *membrillo*, quince jelly. They have been placed on a wooden board and are passed down the table, each person cutting a delicate shaving of cheese and placing it on top of a slice of *membrillo*, popping it into their mouths. I have never tasted a more brilliant end to a feast.

At least a third of the guests have gone somewhere to nap or collapse or sober up. Most of the children are curled up under a large tree in the courtyard, and in between all the laughter and cheer, the sounds of burps, sighs of satiation, and yawns begin to take over. One of the men tells me that they are simply resting, gathering up strength for an imminent second wind.

I leave when dusk falls, thanking everyone. A weak, exhausted cheer follows me. I walk down the hill to my tent, crawl inside, and sleep fitfully to the sounds of distant drunken and gregarious screams from the revived and resurrected.

⤴

In the morning, a cloudbank caresses the top of my head, permitting me to see only the mountains' lowest stripe of strata. I ride by the restaurant to leave a thank-you note for the bride and groom and continue on past stone houses and pastures made green by grey clouds and dew. Cattle munch lethargically in abandoned fields. I feel as though I am in Wales, not in the northwest corner of Argentina. A soft mist has begun to fall and the temperature is bone-chilling. The road is quiet. I round a corner and see a mess of scattered pop bottles set in front of a madonna covered in a slippery moss. I pull over and lean on my handlebars, looking at this makeshift shrine. The madonna is about two feet tall, set into a hole in a wall of vines and moist rock a few feet off the ground. A small iron grate surrounds her feet; a handwritten sign says, "Difunta Correa." On the ground below, a massive pile of hundreds of pop bottles, all filled with water, and a few thick candles are scattered here and there, their low flames shimmering in the mist. There is a rumbling behind me and a truck pulls up. A man jumps out, says hello, and throws a plastic bottle filled with water onto the pile. He crosses himself and mutters a few words. When he turns to go back to his truck, I ask him what this is. He raises his eyebrows in surprise and says, "¡Es la Difunta Correa! Mirá…" He points to the sign.

"Sí," I say. "¿Pero, quién es la Difunta Correa?"

He gasps. "¡Ay, ay, ay! ¿De dónde sós?"

"Canadá."

"¡Canadá! ¿Hablás Inglés?"

"Sí, sí, claro."

"Okay, then I tell you," he says. " The Difunta Correa is a woman, no especiál, like you, like me. She lives in a small village with her hus-

One of many roadside shrines to the Difunta Correa

band and her child and she wakes up one morning and uhf! her husband, he's gone. She waits for him for a long time and then thinks one day, 'I must go to him' and so she takes her baby and she leaves. She lives in a very dry part of Argentina... *el desierto, sabes?*"

"The desert."

"*Sí*. So she walks across the desert to try to find him and it's too much. She dies from the sun, because she has no water, because she is tired from walking. But... " he raises a finger poignantly, "her son, he lives from the milk of her breast for three days, until someone finds him. *¡Es un milagro!* A miracle. And so, she is named *una mártir*, and this is why when we travel we pay our respects to her," he crosses himself again, "by giving her water."

I nod. We are silent for a while. "What about her husband? Why did he leave?"

He shrugs. "To fight in the war."

"Which war?"

He laughs. "*Qué guerra*... we've had so many wars. *No importa*." He shrugs. "He was going to fight in a war."

He walks back to his truck and climbs inside. He starts it up and puts it in gear. He drives a few feet, then stops, and reaches for something in his glove compartment. "*¡Éy!*" he shouts at me. He tosses me a candle through his open window and says, "Make a light for her, *y por vos*." He blasts his horn three times and pulls away, wishing me luck, shouting "*¡Suerte, suerte!*"

⁓

By evening I am in the rainforest. The air is filled with the squawks of colourful birds and the shrieks of unseen animals. I camp by a small lake and watch the sun set behind local fishermen, casting their lines into stagnant water. I go off in search of drinking water and when I return, there is a freshly grilled two-inch-thick steak in front of my tent, still sizzling. I look around and all the fishermen are gone. There are no signs of picnickers or fire. A note underneath it simply says "*Buen provecho*." It is the best steak I have ever had. Lean, gamey, juicy, wonderful. I think of how marvellous it is to be in a place where people do things for one another without hesitation, without the expectation of reciprocation. I think of the Difunta Correa and how, despite her lonely journey and death, she is far from being alone now and I wonder if this is a pysche that evolves in a desolate landscape.

The next few days of riding are equally desolate—it is the kind of riding I like, slipping in and out of canyons, alongside rivers that change at each bend, with lots of time for reflection. I pass through dusty villages that seem to have a population solely of dogs made torpid in the heat. Occasionally one will open an eye or lift its head ever so slightly to stare at me as I ride past, but even that is an effort, and for the most part they just pant and listen to the sound of my wheels rolling past. At night, the cane fields that line the road are set on fire and a sweet, sticky smoke billows upward, obliterating an already inky sky. The crackle of distant flames lulls me to sleep.

I continue riding south on abandoned highways. I ride through the colonial cities of Jujuy and Salta, whose lively, urbane atmospheres quickly dissolve in their outskirts. The sounds and smells of a city seem very far away now. I enter another valley of vibrantly coloured sand and stone, and it seems impossible to me that anyone at all should live here. I pause on the side of the road for a snack and am looking at my map when the first car I have seen in days pulls up. A man gets out and asks me if I know where I am. I nod and he babbles on in a dialect I don't understand. He speaks very quickly and I pull out a word here and there, but he does not seem concerned that I may not be catching everything. I lean on my handlebars, listening as he chatters on. Occasionally he slaps my bike's panniers or one of my thighs, laughing and shaking his head. He points to a clump of ruined wooden shacks along a railway line in the valley below us and tells me that this is the town of Alemania, quips a quick *"Adiós,"* climbs in his car, and speeds off, leaving me in a cloud of swirling dust. By the time it settles, the faint roar of his engine has dissipated and the only noise I hear is the rush of an invisible river. Wind gusts through sand and rock. It is then that I realize I had planned to fill up on water in Alemania, as the next town with water was a good day's ride away. I look down onto the ghost town below and know that I am not going to get water there. Tumbleweed bounces along the railway tracks, squeaky doors flap in the wind. All the ghost town clichés are playing themselves out. Not even a lethargic dog lies on its sad street.

I ride on in the most parched of afternoons, in what seems to be the hottest day I have ever experienced, and in a pathetic display of unpreparedness, I come to understand first-hand Maslow's Hierarchy of Needs, where in order to reach the top of the pyramid of self-actualization, one must move through various levels, satisfying certain basic needs before advancing to the next level. Water is at the very base of that pyramid, and I am not permitted the luxury of reflection (which occupies a higher level) until I can find it. There is no traffic, no town, no house, no one from whom I can get water. The river in the box canyon below, made inaccessible by steep, slick, high walls, is a seething mass of clay and debris. My body is dehydrated enough that it has not oozed sweat for hours. I ride on, losing steam and clarity, wondering if I am being tested because I neglected to genuflect at one of the hundreds of Difunta Correa shrines I have passed in the last few days.

At dusk, I round a corner and see an old-fashioned windmill and, beside it, a farmhouse. I limp into its dusty front yard, carefully get off my bike, and knock on the front door. An old woman answers. She looks me up and down. "¿Necesitás agua?" she asks. I nod. "Bueno, bueno," she says and tells me to come in. She beckons me to follow her through the house, where there are lanterns lit everywhere. We come to a small room, which is completely taken up by an enormous deep freezer. She lifts up the freezer door and reveals a treasure trove of frozen bottles of water. She gives me two large ones, then goes into her kitchen and brings back a bottle filled with cool water that I can drink right away. I give her some money and look around this simple house. Out of curiosity, I ask her if she sells anything else. She shakes her head. "Solo agua," she says.

Un milagro, a miracle. Here, in a canyon uninhabited and unelectrified for a hundred miles is a woman who sells water from a deep freezer, the only electrified thing in her whole home.

I decide to set up camp just down the road on the bank of a river bed that has been dry through all of Argentina's civil wars and coups and fluctuations between dictatorships and democracies. I find a flat piece of ground, lie down, and slowly sip the water, savouring it, until the bottle is empty. Sweat immediately springs up on my skin. I set up my tent and make myself some dinner. The air begins to cool.

A fierce wind forces clouds down the slopes of mountains just beyond my grasp. All night the wind howls and a storm hovering overhead threatens vociferously but refuses to deliver the downpour it holds in its clouds. I peer out of my tent, watching as shards of lightning crackle violently, striking close by. Thunder surges overhead, steamrolling over my tent with a power I have never heard before. When I wake in the morning, I feel an eerie calm, in me and in the valley, the kind of calm you feel when you have been within inches of an unpreventable death; it is as though in watching the storm I have come to understand it, come to comprehend and respect its power, and so it retreats. Not a drop of rain has been shed.

⌒

At noon I am riding through the vineyards of Cafayate, past enormous hundred-year-old wooden vats stacked along the road that act as a windbreak for acres and acres of vines. The town is quiet, steeped in its siesta, but there is a solitary man in the town's plaza. He stands near Cafayate's only park bench, with a large pot covered with a dish towel in front of him and his hands behind his back, looking to the sky as if he were expecting something to drop from it. I wander over to him and ask what he has. He stares at me through ancient eyes and then slowly lifts the towel. Lying on top of the pot's inverted lid are some half-moon pastries, the ever-present Argentine *empanadas*. Under the lid, in the vessel of the pot, hot rocks keep the *empanadas* warm. I buy a few pastries from him and sit beside him on the park bench, eating. He returns his gaze to the sky and waits patiently for his next customer. The streets give the impression of a sudden, apocalyptic abandonment. A breeze pushes through bougainvillea and fans of palms.

I ask him what is in the *empanadas*. He shrugs. Beef, he says.

"*¿Sí, pero, qué más?*"

"*No se.*" He shrugs again and tells me that his daughter makes them and he sells them for her. I ask him if she can show me how to make them. He smiles and shakes his head. He points up at the sun. "*Es la hora de la siesta.*"

"*Sí, sí, claro. Perdón.*" I apologize.

"*Mira,*" he says, taking an *empanada* from under the dish towel and breaking it in half. With shaking wrinkled fingers, he shows me what his daughter puts in her *empanadas*. "*Huevos, y aceitunitas, y pasas de uva, y las especias. Es sencillo.*" Hard-boiled eggs, olives, raisins, spices. Simple. I ask him what spices.

He smiles and shakes his head again. "*Es el secreto de mi hija.*" He tells me that she won't even tell him what they are. "*Delicioso,*" he says, holding his *empanada* up and taking small bites. He closes his eyes as he chews. Eating an *empanada* is like taking a bite of the Argentine psyche: a little bitter, a little sweet, but meaty and substantial.

I ask him why he does not take a siesta.

"*Estoy viejo. Mi vida es una siesta.*" He waves his hands around at the empty square and asks me why he needs to take a siesta when he is surrounded by silence. We smile and we eat our *empanadas* without saying another word.

⁓

An hour or so down the road and a bit off the beaten track I come across a set of Diaguita Indian ruins set high upon the cactus-ridden sierra. Quilmes, as the ruins are called, was once an urban complex of about five thousand people formed in approximately A.D. 1000 and wiped out by the Spanish in the seventeenth century. An air of desertion envelops the place. The road into this place is a rutted dirt path, and the highway that runs down the valley is as empty as any running through Patagonia.

I leave my bike with the custodian and climb up high through cacti and set stone foundations to get a better view. From the top, it is easy to see how the town was organized—where the cooking area was, where living quarters were, where livestock were kept. The ruins seem pristine, as though not a single rock is out of place. A small herd of goats is grazing below. On the horizon I can see the next ridge of mountains that I will ride over tomorrow. A late-afternoon haze dulls the distance between us.

There is a whistle from below. The custodian is waving, a tiny speck between walls of stone. I begin to make my way down, passing a large face of exposed, flat rock with large dimples carved into it. As I get closer, I realize that this rock has a history, that when the Diaguita took smaller rocks and pounded corn or seeds or chilis with them on the large rock, holes were formed over time, creating a rock face filled with natural mortars.

At the bottom, the custodian is happy to see me. It is *mate* time and he is glad to have someone to share his thoughts with. This is a particularly lonely place, made lonelier by the knowledge that there was once a substantial population here.

I ask him if he sleeps here and he shrugs. Sometimes, he says, but tonight he will go home. The storm last night may have done some damage to his house. I look up into the ruins and try to imagine what it would have been like to be here in that storm, where the lightning would have struck, how the thunder would have rolled and rebounded from the mountain face in front of me.

He hands me some prickly pears and a knife. I cut them into wedges and we suck on them in silence. I cannot think of a more refreshing fruit for desert climes: drops of watermelon essence in the texture of the softest, ripest of pears. When the *mate* is finished, the custodian stands, claps the dust from his hands, carefully places his *mate* pot and burner in his shed, and says he must go. He tells me that he will be back in the morning and that I am welcome to pitch my tent in the ruins for the night. Pitch it behind the wall, he says, so that if any of the *borrachos* from the next town over decide to come up the road for a joyride, they won't see you. I laugh and promise, we shake hands, and he climbs into his truck. He pitches and wobbles down the track towards the highway.

The air cools instantly when the sun dips behind the mountain. I set up my tent behind the wall and start a fire. For the rest of the night I sit in front of it, warmed by crackles and waves of heat, gazing up at the sky, feeling very small under a ceiling of so many stars. It is not so very often that we have an opportunity to camp in the ruins of a town of an extinct race and feel humbled by a grander scheme of things.

The next morning I ride into the hills and through a small colonial town where I find cactus fruit *empanadas* sold at the side of the road. The road turns to gravel, and each a house I pass has a small table set up at the entrance to its driveway, selling pickled and dried *ciruelas*, the most wonderful plums I have ever tasted. I stuff some bills into a cash box that has a very friendly, handwritten "*gracias*" sign attached to it and pack some dried *ciruelas* into my pannier.

I climb and climb and climb, seeing what seems like the whole length of the pass ahead of me, making what feels like minimal progress. The road deteriorates to a one-lane, precipitous, rutted path. The sun blazes with fierce intensity. Within ten kilometres, the three cars that passed me at the bottom of the climb are all in some state of disrepair: two with overheated radiators, one with a broken axle. When I ask if I can help in any way, each driver looks at me, looks at my bike, grins, and shakes his head. I climb and climb and climb. I eat my plums. I stop and stare at bare, yellowing hills. The sun casts incendiary rays on my shoulders. I climb and climb and climb. Seven hours after having started out, I crest a steep pitch enshrouded in a dense, frigid cloudbank, pass a small monument, and realize that I have reached the top. I cannot see more than two feet from my face. I lie on the side of the road, pulling all of my clothes on. I eat my last plum and pass out.

I wake from my nap half an hour or so later to a strange sound of ripping and mashing. I look to my right and within two feet of me is a llama, grazing. Directly behind her, a break in the cloudbank reveals a sharp peak smashed up against green sierra. A rainbow arcs in front of me so closely that I daresay it landed at my feet. No word of a lie. I sit stunned, until the llama nudges me out of the way, wanting to get at the grass I am sitting on. I walk over to the monument just as one of the broken-down cars approaches. Its driver honks and laughs and asks me if I want a ride down.

"No way," I say.

He tells me that the name of this road is El Infiernillo or "Little Hell." I raise my eyebrows and nod in agreement, slowly, exhaustedly. He laughs again, shakes my hand, and drives off, honking until I can no longer see him.

The ride down is wonderful. The clouds have closed in again and I speed past misty farms and hills, around hairpin curves into the town of Tafí del Valle. As I ride through town, it is immediately apparent that this place has a vibrancy of its own. In the plaza, a truck with mammoth loudspeakers drives in circles making political pronouncements to the townsfolk, most of whom are sitting peacefully on benches, but some of whom are practising a quick-footed dance to the beat of a tango coming from another loudspeaker that hangs overhead from the branch of a tree. I ride along a dirt street filled with shacks and pull up beside a small, noisy restaurant. Inside, a group of men have arranged a bunch of rickety chairs in a line at the front of the restaurant, and they sit with their backs to the door, screaming and shouting at soccer players on television, giving the fans in a jam-packed stadium in Buenos Aires a run for their money. The owner of the restaurant sees me and motions for me to sit anywhere. The men all turn and look and begin to protest to the owner, who subsequently turns to them, unleashes a harsh commentary that this is his restaurant, ¡mecacho!, and that he gets to say who eats here and who doesn't and if they don't like it they can go somewhere else and watch the game.

"But," says one of the men, "there's no other bar in town with a television."

"Claro. Exactamente," says the owner. "So shut up and watch the game."

He comes over and asks me what I would like and I ask him what he has.

"Have you ever had humitas?" he asks. I shake my head. Smiling, he holds up a finger, telling me that it will just be a moment.

The men cheer wildly at a goal made and suffer more abuse from the owner. "How can she eat here if you make so much noise?" They protest even more loudly. The owner throws up his hands and everyone laughs. It's all in good fun.

He brings me a soft drink and a plate of steaming, stuffed corn husks, then sits down beside me to show me how to unwrap them. A large, rectangular "dumpling" lies tucked inside. I take a bite and taste beautiful, sweet corn in all its glory, bolstered by a small jolt of chili and calmed by a hidden rivulet of fresh, melted cheese. As I eat, the men argue over a play, and the owner fills me in on who's playing whom and explains the play and why everyone is upset.

Half an hour later, my stomach is full, the table is littered with limp corn husks, and the game is over. The men file out of the restaurant slowly, some of them stopping to shake my hand and say goodbye. The owner closes up behind me and gives me the name of a friend who will let me pitch my tent in his yard.

Hector is a big man, who greets me without reservation. He tells me to set up my tent behind the water tank, but before I am finished he has dragged me into the house to have some coffee with his family. His wife is away, but his eldest son is visiting. His six other children are scattered through the house, some catatonically playing Nintendo in a bedroom, others chasing about, asking if they can do anything. Rubbing their heads, he tells them to make coffee for us.

Hector asks me where I am going, and I tell him that tomorrow I will ride into Tucumán and take the train to Buenos Aires from there. We chat about Canada and Argentina: he and his son teach me some Spanish, and I teach them some English. We nibble on hard cheese and membrillo, sip coffee and, as usual, solve the world's problems. At midnight, some of the older children leave to go to a dance in the town next to this one. The younger ones disappear for a few minutes, returning with triumphant smiles on their faces, saying they have successfully dismantled my tent and therefore I will have to sleep in their room. Hector laughs, rubs their heads some more, and kisses them affectionately.

The humility I felt the night before takes a new turn in the face of the unbridled welcoming of a stranger into the very intimate space of family. Hector asks me if I don't feel lonely on my bike. I tell him I have been fortunate enough to realize that there is a need for both space and intimacy in my life, and touring affords me as close a meshing of those two things as I am likely to find. Smiling and nodding, he stretches his arms out and looks around the room. "Sí, sí... and this is how I achieve that," he says, and the children pull on our arms, yanking us into dark rooms where we collapse on creaky cots and dream of llamas in cloudbanks eating membrillo.

Tilcara's Famous Locro

A locro is a type of stew, most often made with meat, corn, beans, and
whichever type of squash is available. The locro in each town
varies, but this is reputed to be the best.

2 lb. squash cut in half (Japanese kabocha is best,
   but pumpkin or butternut or even sweet potatoes will do)
2 tbsp. oil
1 lb. beef sirloin, cut into bite-sized chunks
1/2 tsp. salt
1/2 tsp. pepper
2 tomatoes, chopped
1 onion, chopped
2 cloves garlic, chopped
2 tbsp. paprika
1/2 cup dried apricots, chopped
1 potato, chopped
4 cups water or beef stock
1 cup dried white beans, soaked overnight
kernels from 2 ears of fresh corn, cut from the cob

Preheat the oven to 375°F and cook the squash halves until
tender—about an hour. Remove them from the oven and set
them aside. In the meantime, start the stew. Heat the oil in a
large pot over medium-high heat and add the beef. Sprinkle
with salt and pepper and cook for a few minutes, until it starts
to turn a nice brown colour. Add the tomatoes, onion, garlic,

and paprika and cook for 5 to 6 minutes. Add the apricots, potato, water, and beans. Bring to a boil and reduce the heat to low. Cover and simmer for 2 hours, until the meat and beans are tender, stirring occasionally. Scrape the meat of the cooked squash into a large bowl or food processor and add a cup or two of the liquid from the stew. Purée or mash until smooth and then stir it into the pot. Add the corn and cook for another 10 minutes or so. The stew should be quite thick and the squash should be well-combined. Serve hot or at room temperature.

Serves at least 4 for dinner.

Humitas

Humitas are like corn dumplings, steamed and wrapped in their own
husks. They find their Mexican counterpart in *tamales* and are
a wonderful comfort food. While *tamales* are generally made
with dried corn, *humitas* are made with fresh. Cornhusks and
masa harina, a special type of corn flour, can be found in any
Latin American or ethnic food market.

1 tbsp. oil

1 tbsp. butter

1 onion, chopped

6 ears of fresh corn, still in their husks

½ tsp. salt

1 jalapeño pepper, chopped

a handful of cilantro, chopped

½ cup boiling water

3 tbsp. masa harina

8 cornhusks

¼ lb. mild cheese, like Monterey Jack or mozzarella, grated

hot sauce

Heat the oil and butter in a frypan over medium heat. Add the onion and cook for 5 to 6 minutes, until softened. Cut the corn kernels from their cobs. Reserve two of the cobs and their husks and place the kernels in a large mortar or food processor. Pound or blend until thick and smooth. Add the kernel mixture to the frypan and cook for about 10 minutes, until the corn has absorbed most of the liquid. Add the salt, jalapeño, and cilantro, then mix the water and masa harina together and add to the frypan. Stir well, remove from the heat, and let sit for a few minutes. Take a large piece of corn-husk and lay it flat on a surface. Place 2 tablespoons of the corn mixture in the centre of it, lay some cheese on top, and cover with another tablespoon or two of corn mixture. Fold the sides of the husk over the corn mixture to make a tight, small package. Repeat with the remaining ingredients. Place one or two of the reserved corncobs in the bottom of a pot or large saucepan and cover with water. Place the humitas in a steamer and cook, covered, over medium heat for an hour. Check occasionally to see if water needs to be added to the pan. After an hour, turn the heat off and let the humitas rest for 10 to 15 minutes, then serve with a dash of hot sauce.

Makes 8 humitas, serving 4 as a substantial snack.

Empanadas al Cafayate

Empanadas can be found all over South America. In Chile, they are large and eaten as a meal. By the sea, they are often made with tuna instead of meat, and in the desert, they can be found filled with cactus fruit or prickly pears. In Argentina, they are generally made into smaller, daintier pockets and eaten as a snack.

2/3 cup water
1/2 cup lard
2 1/4 cups flour
1 tsp. salt
2 tbsp. oil
1 tsp. cumin seed
1/2 tsp. paprika
1/2 tsp. chili powder
1 onion, chopped
1 clove garlic, chopped
1 red or green chili, chopped
3/4 lb. ground beef
1/2 tsp. salt
6 green olives, pitted
1 potato, peeled, diced and cooked
a handful of raisins
1 hard-boiled egg, chopped

Heat the water and lard together in a saucepan over medium-high heat until the lard has melted. Place the flour and salt in a bowl and slowly add the lard mixture, incorporating it until you have a smooth dough. Cover the dough and let it rest for an hour or so at room temperature. In the meantime, make the filling: Heat the oil, cumin, paprika, and chili powder in a frypan over high heat until the cumin seeds start to pop. Add the onion, garlic, and chili and cook for 5 to 6 minutes, until the onion has softened. Add the beef and salt and cook for 5 to 6 minutes, until the beef is nicely browned. Remove the pan from the heat and stir in the olives, potato, and raisins. Set aside and let cool for 20 minutes or so. Preheat the oven to 375°F. To assemble the *empanadas*, divide the dough into 16 equal pieces, each about the size of a ping-pong ball. Roll out a piece of the dough into a 5-inch circle. Place a tablespoon of the meat mixture into the centre and top with a sprinkling of chopped egg. Fold one edge over the other to make a half-moon shape. Roll the edges up or press them firmly with the tines of a fork to seal the pastry. Repeat with the remaining dough and meat mixture. Bake for about 20 to 25 minutes, until nicely browned. Serve hot or at room temperature… great food for travelling!

Makes 16 Argentine-sized empanadas, *serving 4 as a good snack or light lunch.*

IRAN

Iran's sensations, her colours, her contradictions, and her pleasures overwhelm even in memory, and when your publisher tells you that you have seven thousand words in which to relay all of what she is, you lie awake at night sweating, worrying about how you are going to accomplish it, much like you lay awake and worried when you were in Iran, knowing that no amount of snapped pictures or scribbled words could capture the country as she presented herself to you: the taste of a white pomegranate plucked freshly from its tree or the smell of baked earth in a long-awaited desert rain, or the sight of minarets of liquid sapphire leaking into her monotone landscape. "Make Iran dance," writes a friend who is aware of the monumental task before me, and it is then that I realize that in order to make the country sway for me on the page as it did when I stood within her boundaries, it is impossible to tell the story in a linear fashion. I have seven thousand impressions of Iran that linger, and each deserves more than a single word.

Picture yourself in a massive labyrinth of covered alleyways built from mudbrick in the seventeenth century, hung with strings of bare lightbulbs. Now, in your mind, gradually fill in the alleyways. Clutter them with carpet vendors, shouting and stacking rugs like soldiers stacking sandbags in trenches, unrolling them and flipping through them, the mustiness of wool and fastness of their colours bleeding into the air; add some old women selling split dried figs and white mulberries, gooey, sticky Medjool dates, chewing and spitting black sunflower seeds held in small cones made of newspaper printed in a sweeping, foreign script; turn an imaginary corner and see boys banging out large copper pots, sitting on the dirt stoops of their father's or uncle's shop, clanging heavily in unison, or women draped from head to foot in black cloaks selling pure gold, in bars or in delicate, thin bracelets and anklets; make way for ancient men bent under mountains of heavy sacks, pushing creaky wooden carts stacked with thousands of pounds of flour or cement or something else through a rippling mass of people, shouting, "*Ya Allah! Ya Allah!*" Fill in the scene with swaths of pedestrians: women in Islamic dress—headscarves and dark shapeless coats—hiding their smiles; black-haired, bearded men in sandals, with dusty feet, a constant murmur of foot on stone filling your ears. Picture yourself pressing your way through the crowd, turning this way and that in the labyrinth, losing your sense of direction immediately but with yet another alleyway to explore, wandering past piles and piles of vibrant fabric, past mammoth peaks of violent, unknown spices, past rooms where men sit huddled over hookas and tiny glasses of tea and where the smell of sweet tobacco drifts out to meet you. Close your eyes and picture everything suddenly in slow motion—a woman walking past you in long strides, her chador filling and col-lapsing behind her in the rhythm of her steps; dark-eyed men turn-ing towards you, their mouths stretching slowly and seductively into smiles that embrace you, hands reaching out and pulling you in.

This is your first impression of Iran. Standing in the midst of a crowded bazaar on the old silk route, saturated by scent, colour, the lilt of Farsi, whispers of Persian air, the sound of smoke being sucked through water, the weight of ancient dust hovering.

The bazaar blurs. Men and women, turquoise and gold, raw henna, clay and stone spin wildly around you. You are its unwavering centre, suddenly aware you are in a place that you never expected to be seduced by. You close your eyes and hold your cloaked arms out, inviting Iran to seep into your pores, your veins, your soul for the next six weeks, knowing full well that she will remain with you for all the days you have left in you.

❧

We are in the middle of the central Iranian desert, Doug and I, straddling our bikes, taking in the vast stretch of baked earth that surrounds us, void of colour, flavour, scent. Some foothills shimmer at the edge of the horizon, but between us and them there is absolutely nothing. It's probably only thirty degrees, but the sun is strong and there is not a sliver of shade for hundreds and hundreds of kilometres. We have been following the plateau for almost three weeks now and have ridden from the mountains in the north to the lush green hills of the Caspian to yellowing, rounded peaks to these salt flats that stretch for thousands of kilometres to the Afghani border. I celebrated my thirtieth birthday yesterday, a match stuck into a dry cookie for my cake. We camped high above the road in a plain of spiny tumbleweed, not a tree or person in sight for miles, watching the night sky almost turn to daylight when all the stars came out.

We look around, as if expecting to see something we have missed after staring at this landscape for days. To keep from dehydrating, we force each other to drink salted water that turns almost too hot to drink from sitting in the sun. We push off, pedalling, pedalling. We ride through nothing, past nothing, towards nothing. The sky is white blue, the land is salty beige, tarmac the only swath of colour stretched out in front of us. At night, the traffic rivals an L.A. rush-hour, but in the middle of the day it dwindles to maybe a car an hour.

A blast of horn shatters the air behind us. A large intricately painted truck screeches up alongside us, nearly running us off the road. The truck is a mélange of green, white, and red—the colours of the Iranian flag. On its back doors, an outline of an Iranian woman is painted with her headscarf pulled across her mouth, the Iranian equivalent of buxom silhouettes of women that adorn mud-flaps of 18-wheelers across America. The truck's sides are scrawled with Arabic script and a large tapestry depicting Mohammed hangs in the carpeted cab between the driver and his passenger, who waves cheerfully and frantically. The driver and passenger hop out, arms filled with fruit. They jabber in Farsi to each other, and while one cuts open an enormous melon on the tarmac, the other shouts, "Shah good! Shah good!" at us, and shakes his hands, thumbs up. The man cutting the melon stops, looks at his friend, and then at us. He shakes his head violently, throws the knife down, and begins to shout, thrashing his arms as though drowning. The two men yell back and forth at each other for a few minutes while Doug and I watch, trying not to smile too broadly. The driver returns to cutting up the melon, still spouting, turning to us. *"Allah! Allah! Islam... Iran!"* We clearly understand their positions. His friend rolls his eyes and the driver wipes the knife off and sticks it back in his pocket. He shoves a quarter of a melon into each of our hands, storms back to the cab, hops in, and begins to drive off, leaving his passenger behind. The passenger runs as fast as he can towards the lumbering truck, shouting "Okay, okay. Shah no good! Shah no good!" eventually catching up with it and miraculously leaping onto the running board without dropping his piece of melon. The truck lumbers off and leaves us in silence, melon juice dripping from our hands.

We crawl into the shade of a drainage culvert under the road to eat. We ride through nothing, past nothing, towards nothing.

❧

In a small town near Persepolis, after the police beat away a crowd that has gathered around us, we are beckoned into a store by a couple of young men. They say that though the police have told us there is nowhere for us to stay in town, we are more than welcome to stay with them, if we can wait outside the store for half an hour until they close, during which time another crowd forms and the police come again to beat them away.

We slip into an alleyway behind the store and follow the two young men through a maze of side streets and a courtyard to a bachelor pad—a high-ceilinged apartment lined with an astonishing array of carpets and typically void of furniture, save for an enormous television placed on a pedestal in the middle of the largest room. One of the men, Abbas, makes a couple of phone calls and disappears. The other, Mehmet, brings out a large platter of grapes, white pomegranates, and fresh walnuts. He tells us that he is trying to teach himself English by listening to Voice of America on his short-wave radio every night. "Bill Clinton… I think he must be a good man, even if he has this problem with the girl," he says.

There is a knock on the door and a few more young men enter. One of them has brought some bootleg videotapes, and Mehmet throws one into a VCR that is hidden from view. "The Flame of Persia," it shouts; it's an old Iranian film in English narrative about the fabulously excessive party that the Shah threw at Persepolis in 1971, inviting seventy-two heads of state to celebrate twenty-five centuries of civilization and to open the doors to the West at the expense of and to the exclusion of the Iranian people. They have brought it over for us to watch, and though they have seen it many times already, they are quite content to just watch the images of opulence on the screen, occasionally asking Mehmet to translate.

Abbas returns, carrying an armful of flatbread and a large pot wrapped in a dish towel. He tells us his mother has made us some kofté, enormous rice and lamb meatballs stuffed with fresh dates. The bread is still warm, and we all sit around the pot helping ourselves to food and asking each other questions while one of the young men starts the other videotape, an Ace of Base concert in Paris. The koftē are incredible—three different textures in the mouth all at once: the sponginess of the rice, the sweet paste of the dates, the salty, bouncy beef, melded together with bursts of orange and cinnamon.

Abbas tells us that his mother made all the carpets that line the floors and walls of his bachelor pad, and that they constitute his fortune. The young men around him say that he is very fortunate indeed. Ace of Base is over and the concert turns into a rap-fest—everyone in the room mouths the words, the meanings of which they don't know. The woman on stage is barely clad, wearing a bra made of hard armour and a mini-mini-miniskirt of chain mail. The men look at me, dressed in my headscarf and coat, and then at her. "It must be hard for you to wear hijab in Iran," Mehmet says. I laugh and shake my head. They ignore me when I tell them that I wouldn't be caught dead wearing a steel bikini. Everyone's eyes are transfixed on the screen.

The saying goes that Isfahan is half the world. The difficult-to-impress Robert Byron was completely taken with the city on his visit in the early 1930s. "The beauty of Isfahan steals on the mind unawares," he writes in *The Road to Oxiana*:

> You drive about, under avenues of white tree-trunks and canopies of shining twigs; past domes of turquoise and spring yellow in a sky of liquid violet-blue; along the river patched with twisting shoals, catching that blue in its muddy silver, and lined with feathery groves where the sap calls; across bridges of pale toffee brick, tier on tier of arches breaking into piled pavilions; overlooked by lilac mountains, by the Kuh-I-Sufi shaped like Punch's hump and by other ranges receding to a line of snowy surf; and before you know

how, Isfahan has become indelible, has insinuated its image into that gallery of places which everyone privately treasures.... Colour and pattern are commonplace in Persian architecture. But here they have a quality which must astonish the European, not because they infringe what he thought was his own monopoly, but because he can previously have had no idea that abstract pattern was capable of so profound a splendour.

When you've been biking through Iran's monotone landscape for a few weeks, Isfahan is a sight for sore eyes. It appears as though nothing has changed since Byron's visit. Here, suddenly, in the middle of the nowhere you have been riding through are the colours that Persians are renowned for, the elaborately tiled mosques, the sight and smell of mountains of spices in the bazaar, the blue sky gaining depth again when surrounded by three-dimensional landscape and by the colours of a million people instead of being bleached out by a searing sun.

We are standing in the middle of the Meidun-ē-Emam just after the afternoon call to prayer. This is the central square in Isfahan, the place from where Persia was once ruled —in essence a courtyard that measures 500 metres by 160 metres, surrounded by a bazaar, a palace, and the two most beautiful mosques in Iran. It is the most marvellous use of public space I have ever seen. We have the place to ourselves. We could run up and down its pathways, listening to our shouts echo off the blue-tiled minarets and domes. We could skip through the shallow fountains or play hide and seek in the arches of the bazaar. But we are speechless, stunned by this beauty, and so we simply stand and stare for an hour or so while the Isfahanis siesta without us.

We are surrounded by tiny tiles, all hand painted, centuries old and unmarred by the sun or sand or pollution, top and bottom, inside and out, in every nook and cranny, every square inch, around corners, on pavement, up minarets that point towards Mecca, on tall domes lit from below by a ring of stone cage windows, beaming their pattern through the dusty air onto tiled floors; one expects to look up to see the entire sky tiled too.

In one of the mosques, a group of Iranian schoolgirls occupies the dome, their laughter echoing off the blue. They coax us to join them when a custodian unlocks the door to a winter prayer hall. He does not want to have any part in letting infidels in, but the girls protest. He turns a blind eye, knowing it will be easier to pretend that something has not happened than to say no to thirty beseeching young women. We descend, deep under the dome to a low-ceilinged hall where small carpets face southwest and prayer stones are carefully placed in bowls by the door. The girls crowd around us for photos. We are a burst of colour in a sea of black cloaks.

Back outside, we walk through the bazaar towards another mosque, passing carpet vendors with brilliant squares of woven wool and cotton: green from henna, red from ground ruby or pomegranate skins, black from ash and blue from indigo flower, yellow from saffron or honey, brown from onion skin and walnuts.

As we are walking under the mudbrick half domes of the Friday mosque, one of the workers points to a door, raises his eyebrows, and smiles. He steals away, but I find a man with a large ring of keys on his hip and he graciously unlocks the door for us. He leads us down into a dark room at the head of which is an incredibly carved *mehrab*, or altar, wreathed in Islamic calligraphy, the words *Allah Allah Allah Allah* everywhere. The man walks over to the other side of the room and unlocks an old, dusty, sunken wooden door. It opens into a further sunken room, another winter prayer hall that stretches back a few hundred feet into darkness. Carpets are laid out facing Mecca, the ceiling descending into white plastered arches like clouds, soft-sloping, their peaks almost at eye level, stemming down from four sides into thin pillars. We stand in awe and recognize devoutness in this room. The man smiles peacefully at us.

At night, we return to the Meidun-e-Emam and sip tea among throngs of Isfahanis. We share pastries and a hooka with them in a tea house high above the square, drawing sweet smoke into our lungs and staring out at the lights lined up like stars, a cool desert wind touching our faces.

We climb gently through oasis towns where coconut palms peer over the walls of old, ruined caravanserais, large sandcastles built from mudbrick that crumble and dissolve after a serious rain. Some are still in use, as corrals, and it is here that I see my first camel, lumbering along with a herd of long-haired goats the colour of Irish setters. The camel is a baby and looks awkward, stepping languorously among hurried goats.

The only sign of life between towns are *ghanats*, humps built from mud that provide ventilation for Iran's intricate underground water-way system, a system that at one point was reputed to employ one third of Iran's working population. Byron described them, aptly, as "strung out like bowler hats in rows of ten and twenty miles." They are a testament to Persian tenacity. As a result, finding water is never a problem in Iran, especially in the desert, and the sight of these mounds causes any loneliness one might feel to evaporate.

At the top of our climb, the road narrows into a small saddle and we see an old man on the side of the road. He is wearing a dusty black suit and a muslim cap, and when he hears us approaching, he begins to sing, a long, lamentful, wavering wail. His voice dips and swallows, bouncing off the wall of rocks that line the shoulder. It is only when I pass him that I realize he is blind. His song trickles away behind us as we swing downhill.

A few hours later we are at a roadside tea stand, sitting on carpeted platforms with our shoes off, sipping *chay* and eating yogurt so fabulously fresh it makes me cry. A car pulls up and its driver and the blind man step out of it. The blind man immediately removes his cap and begins to sing again, walking around to all the people sitting on platforms. They give him change or offer to buy him tea or bread. When he is in front of us, he stops singing, smiles, and says, "*Salaam aleikum*," and bows. He says something to the driver, and the driver looks surprised. He tells us that the blind man asked if we were the cyclists that passed him this morning. "*Balé, balé,*" we say and nod. The blind man reaches for Doug's hand. He tells us that he recognized us by the smell of our sweat.

Riding away from the Caspian Sea coast, away from the last green we are likely to see in Iran, we follow a winding river around slopes of small mountains, through blink-of-an-eye towns where olives are sold on the roadside. We lunch by the river and then climb with a gusting tailwind around a dam. The wind is so strong it whips the wide valley below into a fierce dustbowl, and as we round a corner, tall modern windmills peer over us, spinning furiously. The wind stays behind us and, in violent gusts, pushes us up hills. The traffic thickens to a solid ribbon of tailgating vehicles, travelling at 150 kilometres an hour on both sides, passing without regard for oncoming traffic, which regularly swerves off onto the shoulder to avoid collision. With a wind so gusty, all it takes is for some of it to catch a pannier a bit by the side and suddenly you are on the other side of the road. Doug is in front, near the end of a narrow two-lane bridge, the road jammed with tankers and 18-wheelers going either way. A truck going in our direction swings wide to go around him at the same time that a tanker in the other lane is approaching—the trucks pass each other at full speed with less than a foot between them, the tanker forced to go against the rail of the bridge; sparks fly as its rims scrape the barrier. I cringe, grit my teeth, and pray vociferously to Allah for the rest of the ride over the bridge.

On the other side of the bridge, a car has pulled over and a posse of chadored women stand in front of it, their black cloaks whipping around them in the wind. As we pass, they applaud and cheer vigorously, and one of them holds out a bag of fresh, succulent peaches for us to take.

We pull into a dusty town where grinning kids playfully toss rocks at us. We are told that there is no place for us to stay, but a store owner says we can stay with him. Before we can protest, he has shut up his store and is leading us to his home on the other side of town. We walk through streets of packed sand, securing a tail of a hundred children. Every car that passes comes to a sudden halt, and the people inside stare at us, mouths gaping. Eventually the police notice our arrival and make their way through the traffic jam we've created, asking to see our passports. There is some discussion, but eventually we continue on to the man's house, passing through a Kurdish part of town where the women wear open chadors, showing brightly coloured thick swaths of fabric stretched over their bellies like low, wide belts. Silver drips from their clothes, and large gold earrings drag their earlobes to within an inch of their shoulders. They smile widely and do not cover their mouths with the tail end of their chador, as most women have done with us.

The man beats the children away from his house, and as we are let into the courtyard, his wife, in Kurdish dress, emerges, smiling and pulling us into her home. We talk for a few moments, but just as her husband returns with a large pile of nan-e barbari (flatbread), draped over his arm, the police arrive to take us to "a better place to sleep." We are reluctant to leave, but the police stand their ground. We are told that it is not permitted for foreigners to stay in private homes. The store owner shrugs in resignation, and we thank him and his wife for their hospitality and set off down the road, following the police truck to a gated compound. Once inside, we are pulled away from our bikes and brought to a spare room, decorated only with some chairs and a table filled with fresh fruit and sweets. A woman brings out a large samovar of tea, and with a grin, motions us and waves for us to sit down and eat.

We are at the table with about eight other men, all in plain clothes, and we sip tea for an hour or so, almost in complete silence. It appears as though we are waiting for something. Suddenly the door opens and we all leap to our feet. Two men enter. The men at the table smile and bow and mutter platitudes. We all sit again.

Both of the men speak English and introduce themselves. "I am the finance manager," says one of them, "and this is the director," pointing to his boss, who smiles graciously and inclines his head to us. "Would you like some more tea?" he asks.

They ask us questions about our trip and translate for the others. Eventually Doug says, "Can I ask what we're doing here? We were only looking for a place to stay."

"But you will stay here tonight," says the finance manager.

"Where?" asks Doug, looking around.

"In the guest house, of course!"

"In the guest house."

"Yes! It is our pleasure to have you here, and so you will stay with us."

"Okay." Doug pauses. He leans towards the finance manager. "Why do the police have a guest house?" he asks quietly.

"Police?"

"Yes."

The finance manager looks confused for a moment, then his eyes brighten and he lets out a wonderful, loud laugh. "This is not the police! This is a cement company." I look around at the lush green grounds that surround us, the men in plain clothes, the barricade that was lifted for us when we were brought in.

"But the men who checked our passports, and who brought us here…"

"Security!" says the finance manager proudly. He translates to the others, and the room is suddenly filled with marvellous laughter.

We are led to the guest house and are told that under no circumstances are we to prepare any food. The cook will bring us dinner. The house is set back behind a flowing fountain, surrounded by burgeoning almond and peach trees. Inside, it is like a western penthouse. A large sweeping couch takes up most of the living room. Wall to wall broadloom. Not a Persian rug in sight. A massive table stretches through the dining room. There is a full marble bath and an enormous kitchen, complete with dishwasher. Several bedrooms. Most Persian homes we have been in consist of two or three carpeted empty rooms, with cushions placed at the walls for leaning against. This western décor is presented as an attempt to demonstrate the company's wealth. It is discomforting, complicated. It feels out of place.

There is a knock on the door. It is the cook, with a large bowl of grapes, crab apples, and walnuts, which seems to be present in every home we are invited in to. She gives it to us, leaves, and returns an hour or so later, director and finance manager in tow. They have brought an array of cookies, drinks, and chocolate and spread it all out on the table. When we sit down, the finance manager tells us that the cook has prepared a very special dish for us... Iran's justly famous fesenjūn—pigeon in a sauce of pomegranates and finely ground walnuts.

The meal is wonderfully prepared. There is chelō, Persian rice: snow-white basmati pebbled and speckled with barberries and a few grains that have been perfectly yellowed by saffron. The director hands us a bowl of garlic-flavoured yogurt and fresh herbs and tells us to mix a spoonful of it right into the rice. The pigeon is juicy and tender, its flesh dyed dark by the sauce. It tastes tart and soothing, what I know will be a memory of Iran slipping through my body. The finance manager places a thin golden sheet of dried rice on my plate; it is the crust from the bottom of the pot, the most delicious part, he says, and always bestowed on visitors or important guests. It tastes like a wonderful, nutty savoury cake, crunchy and warm.

After dinner, sucking on fresh Bam dates that collapse into threads of succulent sugar, we talk politics, and our impression is confirmed: the Iranian politic is so complex that there is no way of interpreting it. It resonates deeply in everyone, and everyone, male or female, has a different take. The Revolution is still very much alive, and yet it has met with new competition. Globalization threatens to dissolve faith in the hard-liners' conviction that western influence must be kept out at all cost. It is a difficult enough development to deal with in the West, the part of the world that has brought it on, let alone in Iran, a country where half the population was born after the Revolution and so does not understand why they must be excluded from all that is happening around them.

In the morning, the director and finance manager stuff our panniers with dates, cookies, and drinks. They tell us to call them if we run into any trouble at all and walk us to the barrier, which is reluctantly lifted. We pedal through the streets, and when we reach the main road there is a honk behind us. The director and finance manager have decided that we really should have another pound of dates to take with us. They hand it over and drive away.

We pedal from mountains into wide open plains where nomads are packing up. Huge white tents are being dismantled, masses of rolled carpets sit next to bundles of clothes and food, everywhere everyone is running, scurrying. Boys chase about in circles, herding goats and fat-tailed sheep, shouting, "La-ee-heh, la-ee-heh, la-ee-heh! Balé, balé, balé!" The animals' bells clang dissonantly, drowned in baaahs of protest. As we ride along, trying to remember this feeling and scene forever, a small car pulls up alongside us, slowing to keep pace, and a man on the passenger side rolls down his window and hands over globe after globe of white pomegranates while we ride. The kids in the back seat shout wildly at us, betting on how many we can take without dropping them or falling off our bikes. The car pulls away, the children's faces pressed against the back window, cheering, driver and passengers waving and waving until they disappear from view.

⁂

We are riding along a green river valley high with ripening corn. We pass a succession of tea houses and the auto repair shop that usually denotes a town, then enter countryside again. We leave the main road for a quieter side route and pedal along, listening to the sound of our chains slipping over cogs. Some grey industrial-looking towers appear in the distance. Doug whistles as he rides. The sun beats down and I concentrate on the road. When I pass through some shade, I look up. The towers loom nearby and suddenly they do not look so industrial any more. They have taken on a golden, dusty sheen. Doug slows. We stop in the middle of the road, eyes wide. Here, on a tiny side road, surrounded by nothing and no one, is a place where great rulers lived and fought, where decisions that affected our civilization were made, as unassuming as the tea houses we just passed, but majestic in its humility.

Everyone should have Persepolis to themselves, even for just an hour. We wander through gates and pillars of ruined palaces, up staircases, past intricate bas-reliefs of black marble, walk up to tombs in the golden hills that surround it. It is impressive, set on a platform that overlooks the plains in front of it, reached by stone staircases whose steps are designed for the breadth of a horse's legs, not men on foot, more impressive because where I am standing now is where Darius, Xerxes, and Alexander the Great once stood, more than two thousand years ago.

As we sit on the large steps trying to absorb the significance of this place, the custodian approaches with two glasses of thin, milky liquid. He hands them to us and indicates we should drink. "*Dugh*,"

he says. He points up to the sun and tells us that this will refresh us.
It is fizzy, tart, cool, fragrant with mint and parsley and cilantro.
Later, in his small hut beneath the platform of Persepolis, he shows
us how to make it. A few tablespoons of yogurt, a couple of ice
cubes, enough mineral water to fill the glass, a small handful of
chopped herbs, a pinch of salt and pepper and our energy is restored
to that of gazelles.

At the bottom of a pass, the road flattens and we speed past nomad
settlements. Large black canvas tents dot fields and a solitary child
stands and waves at us. A line of buses on pilgrimage to the holy city
of Qom pass us, honking fervently, chadored arms flailing out of
windows, dropping oranges onto the pavement for us.

Up ahead on the side of the road an old Land Cruiser has pulled
over, and we watch as four mullahs step out. We ride past them and
they shout and wave, their cloaks beating behind them as they run to
catch up with us. We stop, and they approach with handfuls of candy
and pomegranates, grinning, curious.

They are on their way to Qom too, where Peyman, the
youngest of the mullahs, is study-
ing, and have stopped to give us
the address of his mother, with
whom he insists we stay. She does
not live far from here and he invites
us there for supper. Peyman writes
her address out for us in Farsi and
we agree to meet him there.

We ride into the town and, after showing someone the address,
are immediately surrounded by forty or fifty men. Each claims to
know where the house is, each points in a different direction. A
small teenager standing next to Doug rolls his eyes and pulls on

Doug's handlebars, motioning for us to follow. We leave the men to their arguing and somehow slip out of the crowd undetected, roars of disagreement reaching us even after we have rounded a few corners. The teenager takes us down an alley to a solid steel gate and bangs on it. An old woman answers and Peyman pokes his head out from a window nearby. "*Salaam, salaam!*" he greets us. His mother smiles at us and lets us into her courtyard, kicking some squawking hens out of our way. Peyman hands me a proper chador to put on. The general rule is that behind closed doors, Iranian women are free to wear whatever they want, unless they are receiving guests, and even then it is at their own discretion. But in a house in which a mullah lives, the chador must always be worn in his presence.

We are invited to sit with Peyman in a large carpeted room while his mother prepares supper. His three colleagues join us, and though their English is as limited as our Farsi, we manage to communicate. They each show us their official army cards, which indicate that they have performed their obligatory service. One of the mullahs, whose voice is seriously garbled, says that when he was young he fought in the Iran-Iraq war and that his distorted voice is the result of a gas attack.

Peyman's mother enters the room bearing a tray that is much larger than she is. She places it in front of us on the floor and motions for us to begin eating. There are sheets and sheets of lavash— a paper-thin flatbread—and some large mortars and pestles with stew inside. Peyman tells us that this is ābghūst, which is normally served in the bazaar, but which his mother makes for him each time he visits because he loves it so much. It is hearty peasant fare, made with potatoes, mutton, and lentils. He shows us how to pound the stew against the sides of the mortar to thicken it and to release its flavour. And so we sit with four mullahs, each of us pounding away at our dinner, laughing and talking. There is an art to keeping my chador intact while I do this, and my respect for Iranian women increases exponentially. As we eat, the *ābghūst* collapses in our mouths, so well blended that it is difficult to discern the texture of the lentils from the texture of the lamb. Scents of cinnamon and cloves and lime grab onto my palate and linger for hours.

After supper, Peyman's colleagues go to the kitchen to thank his mother for a wonderful meal. Once the other mullahs have left the room, Peyman grabs Doug's sleeve and points to the Walkman that is sticking out of his jacket. Doug laughs and gives it to him, and for a few minutes Peyman is completely lost in music. The mullahs return to say goodbye to us and to tell him that they should leave for Qom. Peyman writes out his address for us. He waits for his colleagues to leave the room, then points to the Walkman, and to his address, asking us to send it to him at the end of our trip. Doug smiles. Peyman bows, muttering prayers to Allah for our safe journey.

In the kitchen, Peyman's cousins have arrived to see him off. A large group of women sits around *lavash* and *ābghūst*, gossiping and

Meeting mullahs on their way to Qom

generally catching up on things. They invite me in. As soon as Peyman leaves, one of the young girls in the room comes over and pulls my chador off my head, removes my headscarf, and starts to comb my hair with her fingers. The women smile and shout and suddenly the room is filled with bare arms and heads. The chadors and headscarves lie in a forgotten heap in a corner. For the first time in Iran, Doug is outnumbered, surrounded by chadorless, headscarfless women. For the first time, I can laugh along with them, speak with them directly instead of through a man. None of us hide our smiles.

$$\approx$$

In Shiraz we visit the shrine of Sayyed Mir Ahmad, brother of one of the twelve Emams. His final resting place is an important pilgrimage site in Iran, and we watch thousands of Iranians prostrate themselves in front of it, while others cling to the bars that cover Ahmad's coffin. Women in chadors and tribal dress wail and hold their children close to them, running their hands over the bars and then running them over their child's face, for prosperity. Men shove rials into the glass case that holds the coffin. Ahmad swims in money.

At the tomb of Hafez, one of Iran's most famous poets, we watch men weep openly and silently. A different type of reverence is being shown. The tomb is outdoors, in one of Iran's justly famous gardens, rung with perfect roses and other gracefully trailing flowers. It is crowded, but peaceful—so quiet that we can hear the water flowing in a small fountain outside the garden.

Doug and I sit on marble benches watching a procession of intellectuals paying their respects at the tomb. It is one of our last days in Iran and we are both silent, wondering how much more empty the western world will feel when we return to it. I don't know what Doug is thinking, but I know I will never eat a pomegranate or melon again unless I am in the orchard or field in which it was grown. I know I will always remember the sight of wind tunnels stretching high above a dusty, desert town. I know I will be disappointed by the selfishness of the people where I am from, who rarely invite strangers into their homes. I know I will remember peering into a bakery and being pulled in by chadored women to the searing heat of clay ovens and having my arms stacked high with hot bread, free, because I was a visitor, a guest, a curious traveller. I know I will remember the light and the sounds and the smells and the flavours of the bazaars. I know the yellows and pinks and greens of the mountains in the north will stay with me forever. I know I will tell everyone that I have never felt safer, nor more welcome anywhere on this planet than in Iran. I know I will never feel so close to an ancient civilization ever again. I know I will remember the blind man singing for the rest of my life, and that I will conjure up the image of a cloud of dust kicked up by sheep being herded down a mountainside by two young boys in the early morning light, and I will hear their yodel to the sheep as clearly as I will hear the call to prayer belted out from blue-tiled minarets in a desert landscape when I want to be reminded of this wonderful place called Persia.

IRANIAN RECIPES

Fesenjūn

2 tbsp. oil

4 squabs, pigeons, or Cornish hens

salt

2 onions, minced

a good pinch of saffron, soaked in 1/4 cup water

a good pinch of ground cardamom

2 cups walnuts, freshly ground or pounded in a mortar

3 cups pomegranate juice or 1 cup pomegranate syrup
   diluted with 2 cups water

1 cup raw pumpkin, finely grated

1 pomegranate, seeded

Heat your oven to 400°F. Heat the oil in a large frypan and add the squab to it, sprinkling with salt. Cook the squabs for 2 minutes on each side, until they are browned all over. Place them in a baking dish and set aside. Add the onions to the frypan and cook for 4 to 5 minutes, until lightly browned. Add the saffron, cardamom, walnuts, pomegranate juice and pumpkin and cook for another 4 to 5 minutes. Pour the mixture over the squabs and bake for 25 to 30 minutes. Serve sprinkled with pomegranate seeds and with some chelō on the side. *Serves 4 for dinner.*

Ābghūst

This is the food of the *bazaaris* in Iran—good, hearty, peasant food for people who work hard. To mash the stew after it has been cooked, put it in a large mortar and pestle and go at it. Let your guests take turns and keep at it until it has thickened. Dried limes are available at any Middle Eastern food market. If you can't find them, substitute the juice and zest of a couple of limes.

1 1/2 lb. lamb shank

6 cups water

2 onions, chopped

3/4 cup brown lentils

1 tsp. ground turmeric

1 1/2 tsp. salt

1/2 tsp. pepper

3 tomatoes, chopped

2 potatoes, peeled and cut into large cubes

2 tsp. tomato paste

1/2 tbsp. cinnamon

a good pinch of saffron, soaked in 2 tbsp. water

1 tsp. allspice

3 dried limes, pierced

Place the lamb, 4 cups of the water, and the onions in a large pot and bring to a boil over high heat. Add the lentils, turmeric, salt, and pepper. Cover, reduce the heat to medium-low, and let it simmer for an hour and a half. Add the remaining ingredients and 2 more cups of water and continue to simmer for 45 minutes. Remove the pierced limes and discard. Remove the lamb and cut the meat from the bone. Chop the meat into large chunks and return it to the pot. Scoop the marrow out from the centre of the shank bone and add it to the stew. Place some of the stew in a large mortar and mash it with a pestle until it has thickened, but is still a little chunky—the consistency of lumpy mashed potatoes. Serve with fresh herbs and flatbread or *lavash*.

Serves 4 for dinner.

Chelō

This is the way rice is typically made and served in Iran, in the home, at the bazaar, and in restaurants. It is a complex procedure, but worth the effort! The crust that forms on the bottom is called *tahdig* and is usually served to guests, but there is often plenty of it to go around. Try to use Iranian basmati rice, if you can find it. If you can't, substitute high-quality Indian basmati. Iranian basmati and dried barberries are available at any Middle Eastern food market.

2 cups basmati rice
plenty of water
2 tbsp. salt
3 tbsp. dried barberries
a good pinch of saffron, soaked in 2 tbsp. water
4 tbsp. butter
2 tbsp. whole yogurt
1 egg yolk

Place the rice in a large bowl and add enough boiling water to cover. Stir vigorously for a minute or two, then drain and rinse under cold running water until it runs clear. Cover with plenty of water and let it soak for at least 2 to 3 hours, preferably overnight. Drain the rice and bring at least 10 cups of water to a boil. Add the rice tablespoon by tablespoon (to prevent it from sticking together) and then add the salt and barberries. Boil for 5 to 6 minutes, then drain and rinse in cool water. Add the saffron and its water to $^1/_2$ cup of the cooked rice, and set aside. In the same pot that you cooked the rice in, melt the butter over medium heat. Stir the yogurt, egg yolk and $^1/_2$ cup of the cooked rice together. Add to the butter and spread it over the bottom of the pot. Mix the saffron rice and remaining rice together and place it in the pot in a mound. Poke some holes in the rice, and then place a tea towel over the top of the pot and cover it with a lid. Reduce the heat to medium-low and cook for about half an hour. A delicious golden crust will form on the bottom. To loosen the crust, place the covered pot in a sink filled with cold water for a minute or two. To serve, scoop out the steamed rice and place on serving dishes. Break the crust into large chunks and place on top of the steamed rice.

Serves 4 as a wonderful side dish.

Dugh

This is a wonderfully refreshing drink sold on the streets and in the bazaars of Iran. The types of herbs used vary regionally... just use what you have on hand.

whole yogurt
club soda or mineral water
fresh herbs (mint, basil, cilantro, parsley, chives, tarragon, dill), chopped
salt
freshly ground pepper
ice cubes

Place a good dollop of yogurt in a glass and fill with club soda. Mix well and stir in a couple of sprigs' worth of chopped herbs and a pinch each of salt and pepper. Add a couple of ice cubes and enjoy.
Serves 1.

MEXICO

Food will make it hurt less... — Nacha, *Like Water for Chocolate*

There is a scene from *The Night of the Iguana* etched in my mind. It begins with Richard Burton sitting on a bus with a handful of Western women, charging down a dusty road. Some small bare-chested Mexican boys suddenly appear on the shoulder, holding iguanas larger than themselves over their heads, grasping them by the neck and tail. As the bus speeds past, the boys hold them out, stretching them so that the iguanas' white bellies arch backwards and their limbs are stiffly splayed. The women on the bus shriek and shiver, frightened by this sudden confrontation with something unknown, but Richard Burton, a jaded member of the clergy who might have been expected to comfort them, only rolls his eyes in exasperation.

It is one of those scenes that perfectly demonstrate the effect of a new environment on a traveller's consciousness: the processing of a division within yourself, how everything about you—your back-ground, your nationality, your loyalties, your ability to be open-minded—affects your view of another culture. It affects how you will see things as you step outside your own familiar places, how you will deal with a country's people and subsequently how they will deal with you. Like it or not, this is a reality of travel; of trying to leave behind what you know so that you might allow yourself to be humbled and saturated by something unknown; of embracing the emotion and images and impressions that resonate within that culture so that you might learn from them as you re-enter your own. It is a difficult thing to let happen, and it is something which tourists try to avoid but which travellers tackle with fervour.

⇌

Jan Morris once said that Mexico has a way of "traducing its chroniclers, so that each seems to be describing a different country." On reflection, I can honestly say that the Mexico I know is nothing like the Mexico that friends and family have experienced, nor do their Mexicos match one another's in any way. It is so vast a country on so many different levels that Cuernavaca cannot be expected to resemble Chihuahua any more than Nordegg should resemble Newfoundland. And yet I am still surprised when someone emerges from a Mexico that is so separate from my own and the others I've heard of before. I sat stunned in the theatre watching Nettie Wild's documentary *A Place Called Chiapas* because I was presented with a view of a country I'd been to seven or eight times that was suddenly entirely foreign to me.

So it is only natural that each person's perceptions of Mexican food be quite different, though let me say that most of the "Mexican" food we are exposed to in our own countries is not Mexican at all, nor is it an indication of the diversity in Mexican cuisine. There is no sour cream in Mexico, nor any of the fancy toppings we are told to put in our stale taco shells. Cheddar cheese is difficult to find south of Tennessee and Monterey Jack is unheard of. Margaritas? Forget about it. I've never had guacamole and tortilla chips in Mexico except in a touristed area. The only quesadillas I've had were simply two tortillas with a delicate amount of cheese in between, just enough to hold the tortillas together when they were heated. No salsa, or messy, complicated sauces, no chicken, no black beans, not even a chili pepper to go with it. Just a wonderfully simple and delicious concoction of bread and cheese. But this misrepresentation is a lot of what the country is about.

Mexico is a place that accommodates its visitors. It pampers them (if they so wish) by presenting them with what they think is Mexican and, in doing so, retains its own culture for itself. But as with any façade, a little perseverance will crack it, revealing a more realistic Mexico, one peek at a time. Whether it is a glimpse of the doorless, windowless shacks on the outskirts of a town where countless five-star hotels reside, or the smell of offal and soggy corn and steamed banana leaves, or the sight of young boys holding splayed iguanas overhead on the sides of dusty roads, this is the truth of Mexico, and whether you are a shrieking tourist refusing it, or Richard Burton embracing it, you are both on the same bus.

⌐)

My first visits to Mexico were as a child. My parents would go nearly every year and would sometimes take my sister and me, booking a package tour and staying in a tourist area for a few days before nearly going mad with the desire to see something more substantial than beaches and hotels and swimming pools filled with other Canadians. I remember most of our trips as driving around rural Mexico, into villages covered entirely in bougainvillea so that the houses looked like they were floating on flowers, or through mountain ranges riddled with cacti as far as the eye could see. I remember being received with overwhelming hospitality, probably made easier by the fact that my father not only looks Mexican but is completely at ease with the place, like he belongs there. This felled the usual tourist/local barrier and caused people to approach us in Spanish, instead of standing on the sidelines and staring at just another gringo family. And they would laugh when they found out that that was exactly what we were, but the ice would have been broken and they would invite us into their homes for a *fresco* or one of their children would shinny up a palm with a machete between his teeth and hack some fresh coconuts down for everyone. These visits taught me the importance of seeking out something different than what is being presented to me as a tourist, and approaching things from a local level; of opening myself up to other possibilities and at least trying to communicate in the language of the people whose country I am in. They taught me a form of respect that has the effect of a boomerang.

I step off the plane on my first solo trip to Mexico. It has been almost ten years since I was here last, and twenty since I was in Puerto Vallarta. I am here for only a week this time (the result of an incredible seat sale and shuffling of responsibilities and obligations), but Mexico has a way of intensifying experience, so instead of worrying that I will not see enough in one week, I'm only worried that I will miss it terribly when I'm gone. Already the penetrating warmth rising from the tarmac brings back smells familiar to me: a salty, tropical ocean air, a lingering stench of fermented mulched corn, a sticky sweet waft of coconut and a mist of bitter tamarind—all the elements of a palate drifting and present in one gulp of Mexican air. I wheel my bike through customs and the officer looks at me, my passport and glances quickly at the bike, returning to it for a longer stare. He looks up at me bemusedly, and asks, "*¿Y su esposo?*" looking around me for a friend, companion, husband, searching the bank of pale tourists behind me.

"*No tengo esposo…*" I say. "*Solo yo.*"

He raises his eyebrows. "*¿Solita?*"

"*Sí.*"

He cocks his head and gives a quick half-frown. "Okay," he says, cheerfully, stamping my passport. "*¡Suerte!*" he says vigorously, which is something I hear often in Latino countries —it means "good luck."

Puerto Vallarta is unrecognizable, though to be fair, I do not remember much of it physically. Twenty years and a lot of development make me realize that I am in a new place; whatever memories

I have about the Puerto Vallarta of 1978 will do me absolutely
no good.

I load my bike and pedal away from the place almost immediately,
riding head down through the bustle of taxis and buses and resorts
and crowded roadways, wondering when I'll be able to lift it again,
and take in the scenery. Passing cars honk and passengers wave, and
within an hour I am past the most ostentatious of the resorts, climbing above the ocean through banana trees and the squawks of gregarious birds. I am alone on the highway, the Pacific behind me, its
last twinkle disappearing through a thick band of palms. At the top
of a long incline, some children race from a cluster of houses to the
side of the road, shouting excitedly at me. I stop and they gather
around my bike, all asking questions at once: *"¿A dónde vas? ¿De dónde
vienes? ¿Solita? ¿Solita? ¿Cómo te llamas? ¡Mi nombre es Alejandro Carlito Morales
Macera! ¿Necesitas agua? ¿Una fresca? ¡Ay Miguel! ¡Vas a la casa por una fresca!
¡Andale!"* One of the boys dashes off to his house in search of a cold
drink. Their questions continue and I try to answer them as quickly
as they ask them, in awe of their energy. They ask if I know how to
play marbles and are shocked when I say that I have forgotten. A
silence falls over them, and their faces grow deadly serious. When
Miguel comes running from his house with a bottle of pop, they
suddenly burst into discussion and draw a circle in the dust. Each of
them digs in his pocket, then tosses clear balls of glass onto the
ground. The oldest, Alejandro, moves to my side and starts pointing
to the other boys, now strategically crouched outside the circle.
Miguel hands me the drink and joins them. Alejandro's voice drops
to a whisper as he tells me who is trying to do what, interspersed
with derogatory shouts at the players… *"¡Ay! ¿Qué pasa? ¿Qué hace?
¡Estúpido!"*…looking at me then and shaking his head as if to say,
"What can you do?" I sip slowly, intent on the game, which is much
more involved than I remember marbles being. The kids run about
the circle, bopping glass from their fingers, screaming, *"¡Otra vez! ¡Otra*

Marble afficionados

vez!" Then suddenly the game breaks up, each of the boys the apparent winner, claiming his own marbles and erasing the circle in the dust. Miguel lifts the empty bottle from my hands as I say thank you. He grins and shrugs. Alejandro shakes my hand, and I say goodbye. I push off and they run alongside, slapping my panniers as I gain speed. They stop at the last house, waving as I ride on, and just as I am riding out of earshot, I hear Miguel shout, *"¡Suerte!"*

An hour later, I sit in a roadside cantina, with a bowl of chicken and *pasilla* chili stew and a stack of fresh corn tortillas in front of me. Two cyclists pull up, wave at me and point to my bike. They are from Mexico City, on an annual week-long ride from Guadalajara, through Puerto Vallarta to Manzanillo. They are only stopping for a drink, but pull out their map to show me the best roads to take. They tell me of a short cut between Mascota and Puerto Vallarta, which is not on the map and which would mean that I don't have to go through Guadalajara, which even they say is hell. I buy them their drinks, and they push off, shouting that the next town with a hotel is thirty kilometres away and that is where they will be staying tonight.

I finish my meal and ride on, the length of the day catching up with me. This morning I was in Vancouver, loading my bike on a plane, and now I'm ninety kilometres away from Puerto Vallarta, on a dry plateau, tired, an hour before dark. I ride until dusk, pull off the road, and set up camp behind some bushes. I drift off to sleep, my head swirling from communicating in a different language, and I know I will dream in Spanish tonight.

At 5:30 a.m., a passing truck rumbles through my sleep and I open my tent to a sky dusty with new light. I pack up and set out through the foothills of the Sierra Madre. It is a lonely day—few villages, little contact—and the only person I see before noon is an old man wrestling watermelons from a field. The ocean comes into view again in the early afternoon and by dusk I have arrived at a lagoon near Melaque, a small seaside town popular with Guadalajarans. There is a campground by the beach, and its owner tells me to settle in the centre, just outside a large circle of cars and house-sized tents.

I choose a spot and lay my bike down, unloading my tent and sleeping bag. My small, free-standing tent looks flimsy, like Saran Wrap compared to the mansions beside me. I set it up, lay my sleeping bag inside, and crawl out. When my head emerges, a ring of people who have surrounded my vestibule suddenly break into jovial laughter and applause. They marvel at how quickly the tent was set up and each crawls inside and lies down to test it out. Most shriek with claustrophobia and shake their heads at the sight of my bike, squeezing my thighs, then having me squeeze theirs. One of the men grasps my hand and nudges me forward towards the circle of large tents. I am pressed through the crowd, passed with shouts from one set of hands to another as though crowd-surfing at a rock concert. I reach the centre of the circle where a woman in a stained apron hands me a plate of steaming rice and beans and leads me into one of the tents. There are three more women inside, tending large stock-pots set on stool-like burners. They lift the lids of the pots and beck-on me over, offering steamy scents of a red chili sauce, fresh corn and a watery pork soup. They tell me they are here for *Semana Santa*—Mexican Easter. Every year, the whole family convenes in Guadalajara where, in a large rock group-style convoy, they descend the Sierra Madre, converge on the ocean here, near Melaque, and spend the week catching up with one another. I count at least twelve cars and trucks tucked in the spaces between eight enormous tents and ask how many of the family members are here. The women look at one another and think for a moment. Forty-eight, says one of them, looking behind her as though she might have missed someone, and the others nod. Yes, forty-eight, they agree. Just family. No friends. Blood only.

Juanita, Erika, Paula, and I chat for a while. Occasionally a child will rush in, be handed a plate of beans, stop and stare at me, look at the women and rush out again. When it gets dark enough that we can no longer see one another's faces, a boy turns on the lights of some of the cars. Their rays converge in the centre of the circle like an imploding sun. Gradually the circle fills with people and the food tent is soon crammed with hungry members of the Cruz family. While they empty the pots, Juanita, Erika, and Paula prepare food for the morning, or perhaps late-night snacking, depending on how rambunctious things get tonight. Juanita mixes together some *masa* for tortillas, Erika chops what seems like an entire 50-pound sack of onions in minutes, and Paula toasts poblano chilis the colour of a bottomless, angry ocean over a flame. Soon the empty pots are filled with bubbling, frothing masses, and the women make me promise to come over for breakfast in the morning before I head inland.

Outside, a few guitars have been rounded up and those who have finished eating sing and play for those who haven't. The best *mariachi* bands are said to come from this part of Mexico, and it is a serious

business even for amateurs. The young men in the group are particularly competitive with one another, each singing and playing faster,
louder, stronger than the person before him with a skill that, where I
live, is reserved for highly paid professionals. The family eggs them
on and even Juanita, Erika, and Paula emerge from the tent to see
what the commotion is all about, raising their eyebrows and
exclaiming at the blur of fingers over strings, the voices negotiating
an obstacle course of notes with confident ease.

It is very difficult to tell who is with whom in this circle.
Children run about from person to person, receiving pats on the
head or a smile or engaging in lengthy conversations. All ages are
mixed and existing on the same level here, and it seems as though
everyone knows one another well. There is no "kids' table," nor
seemingly any tensions or hang-ups or family politics. I think about
my relatively small family, and how my father's side has met my
mother's side only once, and how there is no in-depth communica-
tion within each side, how much our families are segregated by age.
I look around at this warm acceptance, for better or for worse, of
blood, this egalitarian fusion of family where, for a few days every
year, each nuclear unit of mother, father, and children is embraced in
a much larger unit. I cannot think of a better environment for children to grow up in, where it is impossible to tell whose children
belong to which parents or grandparents or brothers or sisters or
cousins because the love is so pervasive.

Fatigue sets in and I say thank you to everyone, which is
answered with a big cheer from the *mariachis*. I leave the warmth of
the Cruz family circle and move in the darkness to my tent. Three
small children are inside, and they shift in their sleep when I crawl
in, making room for me. I fall asleep immediately, thinking of the
joy and comfort Mexicans find and create in family, and how easily
they transfer it to complete strangers.

In the morning I am alone, woken by a tap on the head from a small boy who wants to know if I slept well and if I would like to have breakfast. I get dressed and let him lead me to the food tent. Juanita, Erika, and Paula greet me with hugs and point to the pots, telling me to help myself. *Chilaquiles*, they say and open their eyes wide. They hand me a plate with two fresh corn tortillas on it and I pour a thin green sauce over them and sprinkle them with fresh cheese, onion, and cilantro. Paula pours some fresh cream over top and asks how I slept. Fine, I say, and tell them that the children seemed to like my tent. Were they sleeping in it last night? they ask, laughing. Yes, but they weren't there this morning, I tell them. Oh, they're probably in someone else's tent, or digging for clams on the beach, they say, they'll be hungry soon, you'll see.

I eat slowly, trying to discern each flash of flavour, which, as with all recipes that are passed from generation to generation, is impossible. The green sauce and cream slip in and around each other in my mouth, and I can dissect certain flavours, like *serrano* chilis and *tomatillos*, but I know that what makes this dish so good is not a tangible ingredient. The most important thing, says Tita in *Like Water for Chocolate* when her aunt asks her for a recipe, is to make sure that you cook the dish with lots of love. The aunt thought she was being made a fool of, but I know she wasn't. Juanita squeezes by me to put another pot on the burner, sees the intentness in my eyes and pinches my nose, saying enjoy, enjoy.

About half of the Cruz family is awake, and they gather around as I start packing up my tent and getting my bike ready for another day on the road. I take requests for things to be sent from Canada, gather addresses, and dole out my own. After Juanita, Erika, and Paula fill a few empty pockets in my panniers with fresh chilis, cheese, and tortillas, I roll away, stuffed, chords of *mariachi* songs still strumming in my head, marvelling at the new meaning I have found in family.

⇝

I pause briefly in Melaque, then turn inland and begin what will be a three-day climb through the crags and folds of the Sierra Madre. I ride through small, cobblestoned towns that come alive only after the sun has set, music drifting from one hidden courtyard to the next, culminating at the plaza, festooned with strings of lights and the click-clack of sandals hitting stone, the kind of towns that feel abandoned and shut up during the day—only at night do the doors in the monotone concrete walls open so I can catch a glimpse of the lush gardens and lives behind them.

The plaza is the all-important feature of any Latino town, no matter how small. It is here that all of one's crucial possessions are displayed for approval (and sometimes criticism)—the new dress you bought in Oaxaca, the car your uncle loaned you, the swooning lover you have taken… it is the coffee house of Mexico, and renders the telephone useless. Why phone, when you can simply walk to the plaza and tell your friends there, in person?

For three days I slip up and over the layers of sierra, eating freshly pressed tortillas, roasted chilis, mild milky cheese, tripe and pig's

 trotters, drinking watermelon juice from roadside stands next to the fields. I ride on narrow, precipitous highways, passing makeshift crosses at each dangerous curve in the road, poems for and pictures of the perished attached to them. Each truck or car that passes honks and shouts encouragement, and proprietors of roadside cantinas flag me down to give me water and ask if I need food. At night, I camp on the side of the road, behind jacaranda trees. I fall asleep to cricket legs creaking and wake in cool air and a misty dew, waiting for the sun to turn the mountains blue. I set off before the heat settles in, still climbing.

On the afternoon of the third day of climbing, just as I am about to give out, I pass a shack where snacks are sold at the top of a hill and stop. I lean the bike against a guard rail and ask an old man inside the shack if he has anything to eat. He is midway through telling me that his cook has gone home when he stops, looks at me and the bike, and motions for me to sit down. He brings over a small cup filled with sliced cucumbers and sprinkles a little salt and some dried chilis on them. "*Come*," he says. Eat.

The cucumbers are crunchy and cool and I close my eyes to enjoy their refreshing, restorative texture. I press the cool, empty cup to my forehead and after a moment feel him take it from me, replacing it with an ice-cold bottle of Fanta. A moment later he emerges from the kitchen with a double order of quesadillas and sits down to enjoy them with me. I start to ask him questions, but he smiles and jerks his head back at me, as if to say "Shut up and eat."

When we finish the quesadillas, he brings me another Fanta. "*Métala en sus bolsitas.*" He points to my panniers and I pack the bottle away.

"*¿Cuántos kilometros es a Mascota?*" I ask and he makes the motion of a water wave with his hand. Just over the hill. I take some money out and give it to him, but he presses it back into my hands. "*Pero, las quesadillas, y dos Fantas,*" I say. He closes his eyes and shrugs. "*Gratis. Solo un bocadito. No es nada,*" he says, and tells me to get going before the sun sets. "*Suerte,*" he calls after me.

I push off from the shack and realize exactly how much I have been climbing these last few days. The bike rolls down, down, down in large sweeping turns, and the two-steepled church of Mascota (two-steepled because the landscape in Mexico is so lonely to the Mexicans that they would never think of building one steeple without building another beside it to keep it company), which was just a pinpoint a few minutes ago, suddenly looms in front of me. A man on horseback greets me as if he has known me all his life, and the warmth of Mexico envelops me and I can't imagine ever going back home.

A carnival is in town, and after dark the streets are packed with song, straw hats, colourful sarapes, and children eating cotton candy and peanut nougat in the shape of roses. I am too exhausted to join them, but sit and watch for a few hours, enjoying the atmosphere and excitement buzzing about me.

The next day I ride to the edge of town, where the pavement ends and a rough road begins. I rattle north for half a day, up and down through a cool, deserted forest to a fork in the road and take the path that has "Vallarta – *via cortada*" in faded, shaky handwriting on a paper plate that is stapled to a hydro pole; a road that I will not find on any map. This is the short cut the other cyclists told me about on the first day—a widened horse path with virtually no traffic. All afternoon I descend through lush rainforest and herds of cattle. The only car that passes me I pass again an hour later, the driver waving at me from underneath it, asking me to send a mechanic from Las Palmas. An hour later, at dusk, I am there, quite literally with an inch of dust and clay plastered to my legs. The kids playing *beisbol* in the centre of town tell me to go to the house next to the mechanic's garage, where surely the woman there will let me stay for the night.

Rosita opens her door and regards me with suspicion. *What is this tired, hungry, grimy gringa doing here, in tiny Las Palmas, on a bike, after sunset? She looks nice enough...* She leads me through a hallway and kitchen out to the courtyard behind her house. It is dense with vines and lime trees, perched on a small hill with a grand, misty view of the jungley mountains I have just spent a week riding through. She shows me a cabin set off to the side.

"¡Fernando!" she shouts to one of her teenage sons. "¡La bicicleta, aquí, por favor!" Soon he appears around the side of the house, wheeling my bicycle, groaning at the difficulty of negotiating it under the weight of its panniers. "*¡Ay, chihuahua! Muy pesado…*" He looks at my legs and laughs. Rosita rolls her eyes, but when she tries to lift the bike, her eyes widen… for once her son is right. She shows me the private outdoor shower and leaves me to unpack. She pokes her head back in. "*El kerosene*" she sniffs at the smell of petroleum in the room… "*es por los mosquitos…*"

Once I have cleaned up, I go back to the house and ask Rosita if there is a cantina in town where I can have some dinner. "*¡Baahhh!*" she says vehemently. "*Son todos para los borrachos.*" None for a girl like me. Only for drunks. She points to some pots on the stove. "*Pozole… y tortillas. ¿Está bien?*" She puts her thick hands on my shoulders and pushes me down onto a chair by the table. "*¡Fernando!*" she shouts. He appears with a friend. She gives him some coins. "*Dos Cocas para la chica. ¡Ve!*" She smiles at me and turns back to the stove.

I have heard a lot about *pozole* but never tried it. I know that it is, like *mariachi*, a specialty of Jalisco, this part of Mexico. I know that it is a pork and hominy stew, in which the hominy, or white corn, is soaked in ground limestone beforehand so that its skin falls away and the kernels puff up. I also know that it is usually served only on special occasions, and it suddenly strikes me that it is *Sábado de Gloria*, Easter Saturday. All about the house are cardboard figures, complete with devil's horns and a pointy tail to which small firecrackers are attached. I ask Rosita who this is. "Judas," she says, making a face at one of them. She makes a crackling sound from the back of her throat and wiggles her fingers. "*Fuego, mucho fuego. Más tarde.*" Later.

Fernando returns with two bottles of Coke, and Rosita dishes out a bowl of *pozole* for me, places a few tortillas in a basket, and covers them with a dish towel so that they will stay warm. She tells me that they feasted earlier in the day and that the men have gone off drinking. She pushes the bowl towards me and I take my first bite. Seeing the expression on my face, she says, "*¿Bueno, eh?*" "*Sí. ¡Delicioso!*" I reply, and she leaves the room, going to stand in the open doorway at the front of the house, looking up and down the street. Eventually she spies someone she knows, the wife of one of the men who have gone out drinking, and calls her over. As they gossip in the doorway, catching up on what happened in town today while they were in their kitchens, I slowly spoon the *pozole* into my mouth, occasionally taking a bite of a tortilla, only to clear my palate so that I can taste all the flavours of the *pozole* again in the next bite, as if it is my first. The hominy tastes like a rich, thick corn, and the smoky, deep red scents of the chilis are infused in chunks of pork that collapse into strands on my spoon. The stew has a shimmering sheen that spells a well-fed pig and a dish made with expertise.

"*¿Tienes una huésped?*" I hear the woman ask Rosita, and she peers in at me, nodding hello.

"*Sí, sí… de…*" Rosita pauses. "*¡Aniko!*" she shouts. "*¿De dónde eres?*"

"*Canadá,*" I shout back.

"*Canadá,*" Rosita says quietly to her friend, confirming this.

"*¡Con bicicletta!*" The woman shrieks. "*¿Pero, por qué?*" she asks.

"*¡Aniko!*" Rosita shouts again. "*¿Por qué viajas en bicicleta?*"

"*¡Para encontrar a la Señora Rosita, y para comer el pozole!*" I say vigorously. It is a question I'm asked daily on trips like these, why travel by bicycle. The only way I know how to answer it, especially in languages that I'm not so well versed in, is to say that I travel like this to meet people like them and to try their traditional food. Rosita and her friend laugh, then realize that there is some seriousness in my answer and look at each other, perhaps thinking this is not such a bad reason to leave the comfort of home, to throw yourself into a culture you are not familiar with, to travel.

Eventually, I reach the bottom of the bowl and despite Rosita's insistence that I have another, I turn it down. I have a feeling and flavour in my mouth that sums up where I am and have been for the past week that could be ruined by more, by too much of a good thing. I thank her for her hospitality and after a brief walk through the town, stocking up on snacks for the ride tomorrow, I collapse on the bed of my kerosene-scented mosquito-free cabin and fall asleep to sounds of shouts in the streets, firecrackers exploding and have dreamy visions of effigies of Judas in flames.

In the morning, I sit by the church in Las Palmas, procrastinating. It is only thirty kilometres into Puerto Vallarta, on pavement, and I don't want to go. I look over at a tortilleria, where women like Rosita have been coming and going, walking in empty-handed and coming out with large plastic bags of tortilla dough for another day of feasting. Today is the Resurrection. I hop off the wall I've been sitting on and walk over to the tortilleria, not knowing exactly what I want, except maybe a view of what goes on inside. It is a worn, wooden building, dark inside, and a young woman sits in front of an old scale and an enormous pile of pale yellow dough with a wooden paddle set atop it. I ask for some, just a handful to take home with me, and she looks curiously at me, shrugs, then gives me two handfuls and giggles when I ask her how much it is. She looks at the dough she's given me, then looks over at the large pile she took it from and slowly shakes her head. "Nada, señorita, nada."

~

There's a certain way the sun shines in Mexico that makes me miss it even before I leave. On my ride into the city I think about not having seen a single white person since I left Puerto Vallarta. I think about not having spoken a word of English for a whole week. I think about the contradictions of life here: simplicity on the surface, its depths beset with complexity. How kids play marbles in the dust and how some people still travel from one village to the next on horseback and take relief from the sun in their siestas. I think of the complexities of Mexico, being so physically close to a superpower and the tug of war between the temptation to modernize and the continuation of identity and tradition. About the blind experience of the tourist's Mexico, where the world is all sunshine and palm trees and coconut drinks with umbrellas in them, or the peek behind the curtain that reveals the tightrope existence of a nation in turmoil. But that is not what tourists come to see.

The traffic thickens on the highway, forest turns into fields turn into pavement, roadside shops, car repair shops, bus depots, concrete block housing. I stop at a small *mercado* and spend the last of my pesos on spices and pastes that I can't get in Canada. At the airport, I stand with my bike in the ticket line-up among tanned, relaxed vacationers sporting gold-sequined sombreros and striped shawls. The officer who stamped my passport approaches, smiling.

"¡Hola!" he says. He pats the bike. "¿Está bien?"

"Sí, sí... fue un viaje a Melaque, La Huerta, Mascota, Las Palmas... "

He whistles and raises his eyebrows, and asks me if I enjoyed the food. "¿Y la comida, te gustó?"

"Sí... chilaquiles, pozole,... "

"¿Sí? ¿Pozole? ¡Es una comida especial! Ohhh... " He rolls his eyes and rubs his stomach. "I think you have had a very good trip."

Yes, I say, I have. And he tells me that he hopes I will come back. But next time, he says, don't bring the bicycle. I can, he says, stay with his family and they will make me *pozole* and he will drive me around, show me *his* Mexico.

And I look out at the sun and I begin to miss it. *Suerte*, I tell him, and he grins.

MEXICAN RECIPES

Campsite Chilaquiles

There are many versions of this in Mexico. This is the most prevalent, and simple to make, and is usually served not as a meal but as an *almuerzo*, or late-morning snack. Green tomatoes can be substituted for tomatillos, though any good supermarket or Latino store will usually carry tomatillos. Canned tomatillos may also be used, but will produce an inferior sauce.

1 1/2 lb. tomatillos, peeled and chopped
2 cups chicken stock or water
a handful of cilantro
3 serrano chilis
1/2 small onion, chopped
1/2 tsp. salt
12 fresh corn tortillas
1/4 lb. Oaxaca cheese (mozzarella or feta are good substitutes, though not authentic), grated
another handful of cilantro, chopped
3/4 cup heavy cream

Place the tomatillos, stock, cilantro, chilis and half the chopped onion in a food processor and blend until smooth. Place the mixture in a saucepan, add the salt and warm over medium heat for 10 to 15 minutes, until the sauce has thickened. For each serving, place three tortillas in a bowl, top with tomatillo sauce and sprinkle with some of the remaining onion, cheese, and more cilantro. Drizzle a bit of cream over top and serve.

Serves 4 as an almuerzo.

Rosita's Pozole

Mexicans have several versions of this dish, varying with each region. This is the one I had at Rosita's. Hominy (or *pozole*) is available in most ethnic stores, as are dried chilis.

2 tbsp. oil
3 dried ancho or guajillo chilis
1 1/2 lb. boneless pork shoulder butt, cut into
   bite-sized chunks
salt
2 onions, chopped fine
6 cloves garlic, chopped fine
2 tsp. dried oregano
1 lb. cooked hominy*
6 cups chicken stock or water
8 corn tortillas
1 avocado, chopped
2 to 3 lettuce leaves, shredded
4 radishes, sliced thin

Heat the oil in a pot or large saucepan over medium-high heat. Add the dried chilis and toast on both sides until browned. Remove the chilis from the pot and place in a bowl. Cover with hot or boiling water and set aside to soak for 20 minutes. In the same pot, add the pork and sprinkle it with salt. Cook, stirring occasionally, until browned on all sides, 6 to 8 minutes. Add the onion and garlic and crush the oregano in your hand. Add the oregano to the pot and cook for 2 minutes. Pour in the hominy and stock and bring to a boil. In the meantime, remove the seeds from the chilis and chop the flesh fine. Add them and their soaking liquid to the pot.

Reduce the heat to medium-low and cook for 1$^1/_2$ to 2 hours, until the pork falls apart. Serve with corn tortillas toasted lightly on a griddle, and topped with chopped avocado, shredded lettuce, and sliced radishes.

Serves 4 for dinner.

*You can prepare the hominy traditionally, if you have the time: Place $^1/_4$ lb. dried hominy and 1 $^1/_2$ tbsp. ground limestone in a pot with 2 quarts of water and bring to a boil. Reduce the heat to medium-low and cook until the hominy is tender, about 2 hours. Drain and rinse under cool water to remove the skins. Or, you can substitute 1 lb. of canned hominy right into the stew, though this would be frowned upon in Mexico and does produce a slightly inferior *pozole*. Ground limestone can be hard to find, but I've usually had luck at stores that sell wine- or beer-making ingredients and equipment.

Roadside Watermelon Juice

1/2 medium watermelon (about 2 lb.), seeds removed
fresh juice of 4 limes
2 cups ice
sugar to sweeten

Cut the watermelon into slices and scoop the flesh into a blender or food processor. Add the lime juice and ice and blend until the watermelon is puréed and the ice has been crushed. Sweeten to taste (this is not done in Mexico, but the watermelons there are sold riper and are naturally sweeter). *Serves 4 to 6 as a refreshment.*

BRITISH COLUMBIA

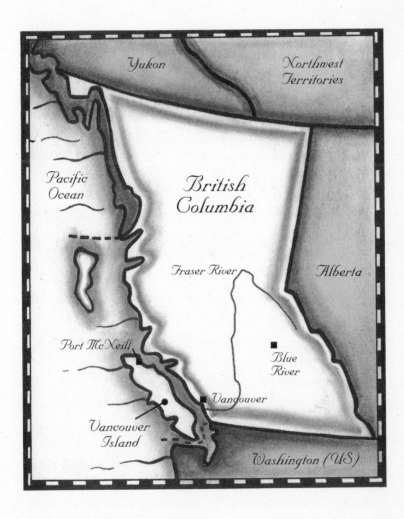

In food, as in death, we feel the essential brotherhood of man.

—Vietnamese proverb

It is a strange thing to find that your home has become a surreal place. This is a natural reaction, I suppose, when one has been immersed in another culture for a while. To come back, not having spoken your mother tongue for months, or not having seen yourself in a mirror, changing daily because of what has surrounded you; to see everyone rushing off to work in a nine-to-five culture you thought you were familiar with and now don't completely comprehend any more; to have been surrounded by guts and noise and belching fumes and cheerful chaos and to come back to silent, structured cities and behaviour, to stand, fresh from the airport, at the busiest intersection in Vancouver not hearing a thing, people and cars floating past noiselessly—these are the absorptions of the traveller who has come home, and this is more of a culture shock and learning experience than Indonesia or Patagonia or Turkey were.

The detached feeling stays for a while. It is an adjustment, a processing of what you saw somewhere else and a figuring out of how to apply it here, at home, in a place you thought you knew well. At first you take a postmodernist approach and ask yourself, "What is the truth of home if 'home' is continually changed by experiences elsewhere?" But eventually you realize what "home" means. Home is where depth counts more than breadth. It is where our hearts lie, where our emotions seep into our every move, where family drives us mad, where friends embrace us, where purpose envelops us. You recognize that you *do* always come back here, even if you don't know why, and that there is value in that. If I cannot find the value in coming home, I am lost.

Andrei Bitov says of travelling and coming home:

> You have impressions. But as soon as you pause and stand in your own courtyard for a moment, your imagination goes to work. For what can be more fantastic than the everyday, or more banal than new impressions? At home there is another dimension of love and pain, another dimension of knowledge, and how can you reveal what your land is, your house, your language—what you are—in ephemeral little scenes? Here you falter, words fail you, and you begin to stammer, your head turning in dumb, bovine torment, your eyes red and meek with love. You come up against a fence. Homeland. Muteness.

For seven years, I came back to the West Coast. I came back to the rain and the mountains because there was vitality in the ethnic communities and vitality in the food there. I came back to the sweaty congee shops in Chinatown that are reputed to be better in Vancouver than in Asia, where condensed steam drips down the insides of windowfronts on soggy December nights. I came back to messages on my answering machine from my friend Mike that said simply, "Let's go for noodles," and we would go. We'd spend the day on his motorcycle driving over all the bridges of Vancouver, eating Szechuan, Cantonese, Hunan, Japanese, Vietnamese, Thai, Korean, Indonesian noodles in every part of the city. I would roll into bed stuffed and wake ravenous and penniless the next morning.

I came back to "The Urban Peasant," my lifeline for six years. I came back to wandering through Granville Island with James, watching him get excited about the lustre of a turnip, helping him dump rotten fish carcasses into holes in the ground at his house, covering them up and planting artichokes on top and then eating those gorgeous, lusty artichokes months later, moaning with delight in their flavour ("It's the fish," James would say, winking).

I came back to working day and night on the set, where a few of us were so dedicated, so moved by James's energy and vision that we did nothing but surround ourselves with food twenty-four hours a day. When we weren't working on the set we were working in other kitchens, or eating in other kitchens. We'd go to Seattle just for the hell of it, or to 49th and Main if we had less time, to look at food, to find something different, and to eat it.

I came back to walking through the streets in Chinatown, where hawkers shouted out the prices of durian fruit and *gai lan* in Mandarin, where freshly caught fish flipped in and out of steel containers set on the sidewalk, where men would swing dough in large circles in the windows of noodle houses, bringing the dough together and letting it twirl around itself, pulling the ends away again and swinging some more until what began as a large lump of dough turned into thin strands of noodles the length of their arm spans. I would walk into that noodle house, order a bowl, and watch them immerse the noodles in a vat of bubbling, starchy water. I would sit down and slurp them quickly and determinedly with the rest of the regulars, vowing never to eat dried noodles again.

I came back to lunches with James, who, no matter where we were, would challenge the limits of my palate and stomach. He would order for us, always asking for something he knew I wouldn't know, and then he'd grin while he watched me eat it. I like tripe. I can't say I like *natto*, a foul, fermented soybean goo that smells and tastes like stomach bile, far-gone Muenster cheese, athlete's foot, and rotten mushrooms all at once, but I will eat it for James, just to show him that I will. I like incendiary *dosas*, but poor Doug was not so lucky. James made a territorial dance around him and as Doug tried to eat the spiciest thing he'd ever tasted, sweat coursed down his poor face and he felt dizzy. He finished it, but tears streamed over his cheeks and nothing could calm his mouth. It was on fire for days.

I came back to Vij's, an East Indian restaurant run by Vik, the nicest man on the face of the earth, who would feed me flavours I never knew possible. Tart fenugreek and pickled limes, perfumy cardamom and real cinnamon, bold and brazen tamarind. He would take me into the back of his kitchen and show me the special pots things were cooked in and would always send me home with a bag of spices to experiment with: nigella (onion) seeds, star anise, curry leaves. Sometimes I would go home and just dry-roast them until my apartment smelled like his place and the woman who lived downstairs would come up to see what he had given me this time.

I came back to the communities up-island, where I watched members of the Cape Mudge Indian Band dig a big pit on the shore for a multi-day seafood feast. Next to a roaring fire, where they were heating stones to put into the pit, they had cross-hatched stakes jammed into the sand, with sides of salmon splayed across them. One of the men ("Call me Shorty") showed me how to gut and debone the salmon, pierce sharp, latticed branches through its skin and attach it to the stake, sprinkling the salmon with salt and sugar. He placed the stakes a good two or three yards away from the fire, in the line of the smoke ("Make sure it's not going to rain for a few days, hey?") and in a couple of days, he said, we'd have the best smoked salmon I ever tasted. And indeed we did.

I came back to my family, to whom food has always been important. My grandmother weeps when I bring her a vial of saffron. My grandfather, after suffering two major strokes and a bout of pneumonia within a week, was somehow alert enough to ask me a favour when I visited him on the eve of my departure for our trip to the Middle East. He wanted me to bring him something, he whispered, as he pulled me closer. "Turkish honey..." His eyes lit up.

Coastal driftwood on Vancouver Island

He calls my sister *mein kleiner Sekt Korken*—my little champagne cork—and if you knew my sister, you'd know there is no more appropriate term of endearment for her. Before she could speak, she moaned at the sight of strawberries, and still does. "Berry" was the first word from her mouth.

The irony is that home provides only a temporary cure for itchy feet. Home becomes a more and more complex place the older you get and the more familiar it becomes. Being away from the contradictions of that intricate familiarity affords me a different view. It forces me to simplify my life and allows me to think crisply, in a lucid vein that I don't allow myself within the denseness of home. It forces me to look at my life and determine what is important. And on each trip, I am reminded once again that no matter what goes on in the world, no matter how destructive "progress" and "development" really are, the waves still do roll in, the stars still do come out at night, silence still does exist somewhere close by, and technology doesn't matter when there is any kind of passion present.

No matter if I am walking past tango dancers in a bar in Buenos Aires or pedalling up a deserted mountain pass in Iran or enjoying *pisang goreng* with a child in a rice paddy on Bali, this truth always reveals itself to me. And that is a comfort of travelling. Some call travel escapism, but to me "escapism" implies indulging in an alternative, hedonistic existence. Instead I find that the world outside the boundaries of my own country is a very real place, complete with destitution, flotsam, and all the throw-away parts of society. I am happy to hand myself over to others, to welcome generosity, to discover those things because within them lie people who lead lives uncomplicated by the pursuit of material possessions and who have not forgotten what makes life worth living, to learn from it.

I will not forget the colourful roadside *sanctuarios* in Argentina, illuminated by thousands of candles. I will not forget riding north of Santiago along the base of the Andes and looking up, thinking I was seeing the peaks of the spine of South America but then slowly realizing that these were only the foothills; that the more I climbed and the more I left the smog behind, the more I'd crane my neck back as higher and higher ridges were revealed, until finally I did see the peaks and there was no room left for the sky. I will not forget how, in the loneliest of landscapes in Mexico, the locals asked beseechingly with tears in their eyes why, why, why do I travel alone? I will forever be reminded that if I ever learn how to speak Spanish fluently, I will have learned how to sing.

I will not forget the scent of saffron in the bazaars of Iran or the exuberant cheer that met us everywhere in Georgia. I will not forget the white peaches and melons of Armenia or how I was made welcome in the kitchen of a Thai woman who bought fruit from a boat in a canal behind her house and showed me how to make *som tam*. I will not forget the sight of prawns swimming in *laksa* or the first whiff I had of Jagjit's *dalcha*. It takes me a while to make a roti these days, but I will never forget the people who embraced the traveller, who took me in, who showed me things that I otherwise would not have seen. These are all things that are important to my life.

There is a certain silence in coming home after all that, of getting used to a different pace, a different way of doing things, of trying to settle in. After a trip, after months of having identified myself as a "Canadian" to others, I find myself, at home, in Canada, abandoning my own culture (Caucasian, of European descent) and living vicariously through the ethnic communities that I discovered overseas: Middle Eastern, Latino, East Indian, North and South Asian. They keep me forever appreciative of the wonderful diversity housed within Canada. That people can come here from other places and feel free to continue to practise aspects of the lives they have led elsewhere instead of "assimilating" speaks volumes about the kind of open-armed democracy that exists here. But I had to go away to realize it, to be exposed to the homogeny and self-containment of cultures that exist in other parts of the world in order to have my eyes opened to the wonderful balance between other places and home that Canada offers in a single place. Food and culture are an easy way to realize that—to recognize a dish or fruit that you saw in Patagonia or Bangkok that you never noticed at home before, to see it proudly displayed on East Pender Street in Vancouver or in Kensington Market in Toronto, where it has probably been displayed your whole life, to recognize a style of music or words from a language you heard in another country and to pull it out of the myriad other cultures that were once blurred to you—to recognize it, to notice it at home is to bring the experience full circle.

Food and culture transcend language, particularly when they act as a catalyst, when they allow you to discover something at home, about your home, as easily as you would in another country. A whole new world opens up to you again and reminds you of what is important to you, that you still have a lot to learn from the place you live in. To open your eyes to the place that gave birth to you, the place that was influential in forming your character... this is paramount to knowing yourself, just as children come to appreciate their parents' monumental, selfless acts only when they mature and are about to have children of their own.

Our past, no matter how recent, forms us and I would be loath to deny it. When I wake just before dawn in Toronto and can't fall back asleep, I would hate not to be able to enter my memory and pull forward the sound of a pre-dawn call to prayer in the breezy air of Istanbul, in the Sultanahmet. I recall how it sounded, bouncing around a small, sparse hotel room where it seemed all the echoes of all the voices descended, calling the city to come and worship Allah before sunlight leaked its way across the horizon. The memory of that distended cacophony jars me awake for the rest of the day and I realize what an incredible labyrinth of culture we are made of, and how fortunate we are to be able to wash ourselves in it: to see it, to smell it, to feel it, to hear it, to taste it.

BRITISH COLUMBIA RECIPES

Vij's Ginger Lemon Drink

This is a wonderfully refreshing drink from Vij's. Its taste depends on
the strength and freshness of the ginger you are using, so you
may need to slightly alter the amount
of ginger juice you put in to get
the right taste. The more you
make it, the more you'll get a
feel for it.

1/4 lb. fresh ginger
1/2 cup plus 1 tbsp. fresh lemon juice
3 1/2 tbsp. sugar
a pinch of salt
4 cups sparkling water

Finely grate the ginger. Use your hands to squeeze the juice
from the ginger into a small bowl, making sure there is no
ginger pulp in the juice. Combine 4 teaspoons of the ginger
juice with the lemon juice, sugar and salt. Stir well and pour
equal amounts of the mixture into 4 glasses. Stir 1 cup of
sparkling water into each glass.
Serves 4.

Mabo Dofu

This is the Japanese equivalent of meat and potatoes. A version of it is served at my favourite restaurant in Vancouver, the only place I know of in Canada that serves Japanese peasant food with a big note attached to each menu that says "No sushi, o.k?"

1 inch fresh ginger
2 cloves garlic
1 red chili, chopped, or a large pinch of
  dried chili flakes
1 tsp. rice vinegar
2 tbsp. oil
1 lb. ground pork or beef
1 lb. tofu, cut into bite-sized pieces
3 green onions, chopped
3 tbsp. soy sauce
1 cup water
1 tsp. cornstarch

In a mortar or food processor, purée the ginger, garlic, chili, and rice vinegar into a paste. Heat the oil in a wok over medium-high heat. Add the paste and cook for 2 minutes, until it is fragrant. Add the pork and cook for 4 to 5 minutes, breaking it up, until it is browned all over. Stir the tofu and green onions in carefully and cook for another 2 to 3 minutes. Mix the soy, cornstarch and water together, and pour the mixture over the tofu and pork. Bring it to a boil and let it simmer for a minute or two, until thickened. Serve immediately, over plain, short-grain rice.

Serves 4 for dinner.

Johnson Strait Smoked Salmon

This is a rough-and-ready version of smokehouse salmon. Do it outside, when the weather's going to be good for a couple of days.

2 whole sides of salmon, gutted and deboned, skin on
rock salt
white sugar
wooden stakes (cedar are great, but any kind will do)

Make a fire, using a fragrant hardwood, like oak, beech, mesquite, apple, or cherry and have a good day or two's supply. While the fire gets going, take a long stake (4 to 5 feet long) and make a cross-hatched pattern at one end of it with the other stakes. You are basically building a grid that the salmon will lie on. Secure the salmon to the cross-hatched stakes, either by piercing the flesh, or by attaching it with needle and fishing line or wire. Lay the salmon flat and coat with salt and sugar. Let everything dissolve into the salmon while the fire gets hot, about half an hour. Jam the long stake into the ground (cross-hatched end up) about 2 yards from the fire, in the line of smoke. Tend the fire occasionally, making sure that it is a pretty constant temperature, and that the salmon is still in the line of smoke. Leave for 18 to 24 hours, depending on the heat of the fire and the thickness of the salmon. Let the salmon cool in a dry place, indoors or out, for 4 to 6 hours, and then enjoy.
Makes 2 sides of smoked salmon.

SUGGESTED READINGS AND VIEWINGS

GEORGIA

Bitov, Andrei. "Choosing a Location: Georgian Album." *A Captive of the Caucasus.* New York: Farrar Straus Giroux, 1992.

Djordjadze Nana. *A Chef in Love.* 99 min. Sony Picture Classics, 1996. Film.

Dumas, Alexandre. *Adventures in Caucasia.* Philadelphia: Chilton Books, 1962.

Goldstein, Darra. *The Georgian Feast.* New York: Harper Collins, 1993.

Gould, Kevin. "Cult of the Vine." *Food Illustrated* (September 1999): pp. 88–95.

MEXICO

Colle, Marie-Pierre, and Guadalupe Rivera. *Frida's Fiestas.* New York: Clarkson Potter Publishers, 1994.

Esquivel, Laura. *Like Water for Chocolate.* New York: Doubleday, 1992.

Knickerbocker, Peggy. "The Seven Wonders of Oaxaca." *Saveur* (Summer 1994): pp. 54–66.

Lawrence, D.H. *Mornings in Mexico.* London: Martin Secker and Warburg, 1927.

Ortiz, Elizabeth Lambert. *The Festive Food of Mexico.* London: Kyle Cathie Ltd., 1992.

IRAN

Batmanglij, Najmieh. *New Food of Life: Ancient Persian and Modern Iranian Cooking and Ceremonies.* Washington, D.C.: Mage 1992.

Byron, Robert. *The Road to Oxiana.* London: Picador, 1994.

Gould, Kevin. "Grains of Truth." *Food Illustrated* (September 1998): p. 48–49.

Kiarostami, Abbas. *The Wind Will Carry Us.* 118 min. MK2, 1999. Film.

Makhmalbaf, Mohsen. *Gabbeh.* 75 min. MK2, 1996. Film.

Montaigne, Fen. "Iran: Testing the Waters of Reform." *National Geographic* (July 1999): pp. 2–33

INDONESIA

Hendy, Alastair. "Indonesian Flavours." *Food Illustrated* (November 1998): pp. 34–43.

Peterson, David, and Joan. *Eat Smart in Indonesia.* Madison, WI: Gingko Press, 1997.

Weir, Peter. *The Year of Living Dangerously.* 115 min. MGM, 1982. Film.

PATAGONIA

Chatwin, Bruce. *In Patagonia*. London: Jonathan Cape Ltd., 1977.

Chatwin, Bruce, and Paul Theroux. *Patagonia Revisited*. London: Michael Russell, 1985.

Darwin, Charles. *The Voyage of the Beagle*. London: Dent, 1975.

Wheeler, Sara. *Travels in a Thin Country*. London: Little Brown and Co., 1994.

Whitaker, Neale. "Viva Argentina." *Food Illustrated* (February 1999): pp. 36–45.

THAILAND

Connelly, Karen. *Dream of a Thousand Lives: A Sojourn in Thailand*. Seattle: Seal Press, 2001.

TURKEY & ARMENIA

Basan, Ghillie. *Classic Turkish Cooking*. New York: St. Martin's Press, 1997.

Bitov, Andrei. "Lessons of Armenia: Journey out of Russia." *A Captive of the Caucasus*. New York: Farrar Straus Giroux, 1992.

Egoyan, Atom. *Calendar*. 85 min. Ego Film Arts, 1993. Film.

Morris, Jan. "City of Yok: Istanbul, 1978." *Destinations*. New York: Oxford University Press/Rolling Stone, 1980.

Peterson, David and Joan. *Eat Smart in Turkey*. Madison, WI: Gingko Press, 1996.

Selby, Bettina. *Beyond Ararat: A Journey Through Eastern Turkey*. London: Abacus, 1993.

TourArmenia: http://www.arminco.com/tourarmenia. Web site.

MALAYSIA & SINGAPORE

Gold, Jonathan. "Singapore Street Food." *Saveur* (Sept./Oct. 1995): pp. 74–86.

Willoughby, John. "Asian Greenery." *Saveur* (Mar./Apr. 1995): pp. 66–76.

NORTHERN ARGENTINA

Iyer, Pico. "La Dolce Vita Meets 'The Hyper,'" *Falling Off the Map*. New York: Alfred A. Knopf, 1993.

McCabe, Connie. "The Capital of Beef." *Saveur* (May/June 1999): pp. 68–82.

Olivera, Hector. *Funny Little Dirty War*. 80 min. Connoisseur Video, 1982. Film.

GENERAL

Jaffrey, Madhur. *A Taste of the Far East*. New York: Carol Southern Books, 1993.

Kaplan, Robert D. *The Ends of the Earth: A Journey to the Frontiers of Anarchy*. New York: Random House, 1996.

Sterling, Richard, ed. *Traveller's Tales: Food—A Taste of the Road*. San Francisco: Traveller's Tales, Inc. 1996.